I was born in Wolverhampton in 1944 but lived my early years in Hessle near Kingston upon Hull. At school I developed a keen interest in writing and won several awards. In 1962 I joined the Royal Air Force and it was at RAF Patrington, East Yorkshire where I met my husband, Lou. We moved to Newcastle upon Tyne in 1966, and I have lived here ever since. We have two children, three grandsons and a great granddaughter, the latter being a pure delight!

My first book, *Prisoner on Prescription*, (a true account of successful tranquilliser withdrawal) was first published in 1990 and is still on sale to this day.
The Truth? is my fourth book and was told to me by Louis Llewellyn Jones…

Born in Newcastle upon Tyne in 1943, he also joined the RAF in the early 1960s, where he now resides. We are now divorced but remain good friends and for several years he worked and lived in Scotland which is where he unearthed this amazing story.

The narrator – Louis Llewellyn Jones

THE TRUTH?

Also by the same author

Capricorn Moon (2003)
(Vanguard Press)
ISBN: 9781 84386 022 8

Prisoner on Prescription
(Headway Books 1990)
Benzobookreview.com
ISBN 0951394526

HEATHER JONES

THE TRUTH?
Narrated by Louis Llewellyn Jones

Vanguard Press

VANGUARD PAPERBACK

© Copyright 2021
Heather Jones

A CIP catalogue record for this title is
available from the British Library.

ISBN 978 1 80016 277 8

*Vanguard Press is an imprint of
Pegasus Elliot MacKenzie Publishers Ltd.*
www.pegasuspublishers.com

Some characters' names have been changed to protect their identity.

First Published in 2013

**Vanguard Press
Sheraton House Castle Park
Cambridge England**

Printed & Bound in Great Britain

Dedication

To Louise and Paul… my babies… my rock.

Heather Jones

***

In loving memory of my mother, Winifred Jones.
She taught me how to 'trust' the hard way!

To my two gifted children… Louise and Paul…
thank you for your contribution to this book.

Also to John and Callum for all their help with
the historic research.

Thanks, lads!

Louis Llewellyn Jones (Narrator)

Acknowledgement

Cover by courtesy of Paul William Llewellyn
Jones

(turnipheadpictures)

LE NOUVEAU TESTAMENT

DE NOSTRE SEIGNEUR

JESUS-CHRIST,

Traduit sur l'ancienne Edition Latine, corrigée par le commandement du Pape Sixte V.

Et publiée par l'autorité du Pape Clement VIII.

Par le R. P. DENYS AMELOTE, Prêtre de l'Oratoire, Docteur en Theologie.

A PARIS,

Chez PIERRE HERISSANT, ruë neuve Nôtre - Dame , aux trois Vertus.

M. DC. XCIX.

Avec Approbations & Privilege du Roy.

The following day,
I returned to the bookshop and bought it.

FOREWORD

This is a true account of one man's life-changing experience. An account so compelling it had to be told.

Lou Jones – a raised 'down to earth' Geordie – whilst living in Scotland, stumbled across this amazing experience purely by chance. Personal circumstances drew him into an ancient world of mystical Christian knights, hidden holy artefacts and a secret dynasty that would rock the foundations of Christianity and what it stands for today.

Many books have been written about this fascinating tale. Be it myth, legend or fact, many people have tried to solve this age-old enigma. But this is not a fictional novel or history book – it is an actual account of one ordinary man's journey into a world of intrigue, deceit and bloodshed. His findings changed his life forever. His findings are in his honest and humble opinion… the truth.

I will leave the rest and decision up to you.

PROLOGUE

As tradition stands, I can honestly say that I can lay claim – one hundred percent – to being a true 'Geordie'. Like the Cockneys born within the sound of the Bow Bells, we here in Newcastle declare that to have this right, one's birth has to be within a stone's throw from the north banks of the River Tyne. So my arrival into the world on September 20th, 1943, in a typical two-up two-down, back to back terraced house just off the famous Scotswood Road was – if I was to hazard a guess – just about spitting distance from the great river!

The area was colourful, gritty and tough. Living was hard and loving even harder. And as some would say – not the easiest start in life. But it was a community where folk stuck together; fighting and comradeship ran alongside each other and you were never without a friend.

My father was a southern man serving with the Black Watch during World War Two. My mother worked at Vickers Armstrong, the famous tank and ammunitions factory, doing 'her bit' for the war cause against Adolf Hitler. They met at a tea dance whilst he was here on leave and after a whirlwind courtship, they married in 1941. It was in October 1946, shortly after being demobbed from the army, following – from what I have been led to believe – quite a volatile argument, he walked out. He never came back. My sister, Florence was born three months later and I was just three years old.

Winifred, my mother (God rest her soul) now had to go to work. She had no option; we had to be clothed and fed. No single parent benefit in those days, I'm afraid. All I can say is thank God for the ever present 'Ticket Man'. Because with the help from him and clothing coupons we were two of the best dressed kids in the street!

As war work was no longer necessary, she gained employment as a barmaid in the notorious pubs along 'our bit' of Scotswood Road. I believed she pulled pints in most of them and – trust me – there were many! One on the corner of every street, in fact!

Because of my mother's absence during licensing hours, I spent most of my early years with my Nana. Big in stature and big in heart; unofficial local midwife; counsellor; everybody's friend – Florrie Wilson was the essence of what Scotswood characters were made from. I absolutely adored her!

My childhood years were simple, carefree ones. When not at school, my friends and I would spend our days playing football in the street, using the lamp-posts as goal posts. Sometimes this would go on 'til eleven o'clock at night, using the streetlights to see what we were doing! Not a pastime that would go down well with the neighbours these days, I'm afraid!

It was usually around the time when the siren for the end of the working day would sound that we'd sit at the roadside waiting for the men to leave Armstrong's factory.

"Do you have any bait left, mister?" we would ask with a mischievous grin. Mucky faces, hands and knees; we were the street-urchins of our day. Sometimes they would send us away with a flea in our ear for our cheek, but other times – if we were lucky – we would get a smile and a curled up jam sandwich!

Saturday morning was time for the pictures. Armed with empty pop bottles we would exchange them for pennies at the corner shop and then head off to the local cinema. A morning spent laughing with Abbott and Costello and Laurel and Hardy or cheering along Audie Murphy, wearing his white hat and leading the cavalry in the Wild West, was a morning well spent!

Running along Scotswood Road and putting half pennies in the tram lines and then wait for a tram to come along to bend them, was also great fun. An offence worthy of an 'asbo' these days, surely!? My mother would find out what I had been up to and set up chase. I can still see her now!

She would beckon me from afar, standing with one hand on her hip.

"Come here, yer little sod!" she would holler. "I'm not running after you!"

"No!" I would shout back with a scowl. "You'll hit me!"

"No – I won't. Just come here!"

"Y-you promise?" I wasn't sure. "You won't hit me?"

She would nod her head, reassuringly. "Yes, I promise." Her voice had softened slightly, but I still wasn't convinced.

"*Re – eally* promise?" I would ask tentatively.

"Yes*, really* promise."

I would then approach her with extreme caution – mixed with a sort of wavering trust.

"*Ow*, Mam!" I would howl, at the same time clutching my smarting ear that was stinging from her hard hand. "*You* promised! You *know* you did!" I really should have known better. Tricked by your own mother!

"That will teach you not to believe everything that folk tell you!" she said, as she walked away. "And by the way, *don't* do it again!"

But I did. And when she found out, we would go through the same scenario over and over again. Naïve as I was then to adult tactics of parenthood – I, trustingly would believe her. It happened every time.

'Don't believe everything you are told!' Little did I realise then how true my mother's words were. And it was these words that would serve my enquiring mind well in the many years ahead.

We left Scotswood Road at the beginning of the house clearances in the early fifties. My mother made sure that she was one of the first people to put their name down for a brand new council property. With an inside toilet and bath, it was like living in a luxury hotel! My sister and I were really impressed! A new home brought with it a new school and new friendships and subsequently, a few years later, a new job. An apprentice electrician was a respected trade well enough, but not one that I was happy in. As the next two years progressed I became increasingly dissatisfied with life – there had to be more to it than this. I needed to set my sights in a different direction.

**

In June 1961 I enrolled into the Royal Air Force and changed my life forever.

**

Watching a solitary blip rotate slowly round a radar screen in the middle of the night, is not the most scintillating of experiences.

It was the 17th of November, 1963 and I was stationed at the remote radar base RAF Saxa Vord; weather 41°F; visibility good; time 02.00 hours. 'Saxa', as it was called by those in the force was famed for being situated on the tip of the northernmost inhabited island of Great Britain, the Shetland Isle of Unst. Treeless and windswept and boasting unspoilt beaches, it was a place where wildlife greatly outnumbered people. Wildly beautiful, but isolated and very much outdated, with the chief access being a very rough sea passage by courtesy of the aptly named ferryboat the MV *St. Clair* from Aberdeen, it was like going back fifty years in time! With a definite lack of female company (no WRAF personnel allowed in those days, I'm afraid), we had to make our own entertainment. Don't forget, this was the start of the swinging sixties, so this was not one of the favourite postings for a trendy, lustful young airman, I can assure you.

It was now 02.30 hours and time was passing slowly. At that moment all was quiet in the northern skies, with no military or civilian flight plans logged. It could have been so easy to let your mind drift into more exciting territories, but we were in the middle of the Cold War with our main adversary – as the crow flies, so to speak – not that far away! Vigilance and readiness for immediate action were paramount at all times.

I yawned, stretched and then sighed. It was going to be a long night.

My mind eventually succumbed to the boredom and began to wander onto more stimulating thoughts. It was 02.45 hours when the unexpected blip appeared on the radar screen, seemingly from nowhere.

Aha, what's this? Immediately my military-trained mind kicked into military-mode gear.

Bloody 'Ruskies' snooping about! M'mm, you think you're clever, don't you? I said to myself with just a touch of a satisfied smirk. But I've seen you! I then proceeded to track the position and height of the offending aircraft at the same time as reporting to my senior officer.

"Get its speed!" the officer's voice instructed through my headphones after hearing my report.

I immediately obeyed the command. "Jesus!" I exclaimed under my breath, not believing what I was seeing on the screen.

"E-rr-m, 3500 mile per hour, sir," I replied, hesitatingly. This was certainly no Russian fighter: not any fighter, in fact. No aircraft known to man could fly at that speed. A meteorite, maybe? But that possibility that my sensible head was throwing at me was soon shattered. The blip changed direction and then as quickly as it came it disappeared off the screen.

"Keep it tracked!" the officer ordered, at the same time as the unexpected happened.

"I can't, sir," I responded with a puzzled frown. "It's gone… disappeared."

There was a short silence down the line.

"Do you want to report this?" the officer asked. "Do you want to report an UFO?"

I thought for a moment before I gave him my reply.

"Negative, sir. I do not."

Over fifty years later, however, I am now – in hindsight – reporting it!

***

This was my first encounter with the 'unexplained' and now my ever-questioning and sceptical brain would not let it go. What was it? Where did it go? And where the hell did it come from? Were there other worlds or galaxies out there far more advanced than us? This couldn't be possible in our universe – or could it? These questions were buzzing around my head like bees around a honey pot. Space travel was still very much in its infancy in 1963. There had been no moon landing as yet. We were still in the era where we were really not sure whether there was life on Mars or not!

A few days later, on November 22nd, something happened that put an abrupt halt on any thoughts or speculations I had on UFOs, aliens and other galaxies. John F. Kennedy, the president of the USA had been assassinated in Dallas, Texas and the whole of the British military had been placed on red alert.

***

It was in the spring of 1964 that I left Saxa Vord and returned to my old stamping ground of RAF Patrington. I don't know what drew me back to this small, farming village near the Yorkshire coast. I was first stationed there in 1961 after finishing training, so maybe it was because I was going back to a familiar place – a place which I held in high regard.

"There's nowt as friendly as Yorkshire folk", is the expression. I have to say, that in my experience, this is very true! Situated just under twenty miles east of Kingston upon Hull and near the quaint seaside town of Withernsea, Patrington was not quite the 'hot-spot' of life in the 1960s! Nevertheless, it held a 'soft spot' in my heart!

A familiar place had brought with it familiar people. People who I had forged strong friendships with before my tour of the Shetlands. There were new people too. However, there was one new person in particular – someone who I would spend my life with for many years to come. My future wife and the mother of my children.

It was the summer of '64 and I had fallen love.

After leaving the RAF in 1966, my wife, my daughter, Louise and I moved backed to my home town of Newcastle upon Tyne. The birth of my son, Paul, followed three years later. This was the summer of 1969, just a few weeks prior to the Apollo 11 moon landing. Despite not being outwardly involved with outer space and unexplained extra-terrestrial happenings, my interest in other planets, worlds or galaxies had not been forgotten. Just put on ice for the time being! So when the opportunity came to watch this historical event live on television in the middle of the night, I volunteered to do the two o'clock night feed! At 02.56 am GMT, July 21st, 1969, Neil Armstrong opened the hatch of the lunar module and clamoured slowly down the steps onto the surface of the moon and Paul, my baby son, responded with a massive burp! It was our first father and son moment. It is such a shame he was just six weeks old and didn't appreciate it!

After several attempts at different occupations, I began working as a salesman in a large furniture and carpet company in the city centre. Promotion came pretty quickly which was followed by a new house, new car and a cat! Very much the average family, one could say!

It goes without saying, that when your children go to school, the build-up to Christmas brings with it the traditional school nativity play, with pupils of a very young age all vying for the star roles. Now with my family – if my memory serves me well – this was not the case. My grandson, who at the tender age of six, declared strongly that he didn't want to play 'Joseph'. He didn't like Mary. She was bossy and pushed him over. He wanted to be a camel instead! All I can say is, thank goodness that Joseph didn't have a speaking part! His face though was a picture. As the famous saying goes… it spoke a thousand words. It was one of those moments where you had to be there!

The nativity scene, with the baby Jesus in the manger and the shepherds and three kings being guided to the stable by the star of Bethlehem has been a favourite with old and young alike for many years. However, with my experience of suspected UFOs and other life in other worlds, the whole theory of the nativity still had me wondering.

"The star of Bethlehem could have been a spaceship," I would suggest to my wife. "The Archangel Gabriel could have been a spaceman from a dynasty from another planet or even galaxy. He could have impregnated her." Bold words in those days: blasphemous even!

"Heathen!" she would exclaim in a rebuking but joking manner.

"No, seriously," I insisted. "It makes sense. I'm not saying that Jesus did not exist. He did. But the 'nativity' – the 'crucifixion' – especially the crucifixion – there is something about the whole story that is not right."

She shook her head with disbelief. "You are only saying that because you are an atheist," she remarked with a dry smile.

"No," I replied. "Not an atheist. An agnostic. That is something completely different." As always – like a modern day 'Doubting Thomas' – I needed proof. However, before this could happen, I would have to be patient. I still had a lot more living and learning to get through!

***

It was during 1982 that I decided to apply my knowledge of the furniture and carpet trade to my best advantage and opened up my own carpet company. I ran a respected and successful business for fourteen years until the recession of late 1995. It took us all by surprise, especially small businesses and one year later – after a long and painful struggle – I had no choice but to bring it to a close. During this time it was not just my company that had collapsed but my marriage had suffered too and then when a third party entered my wife's life, we separated. Bizarrely though, we still remained close and continued to play a part in each other's lives. In fact, it was she who suggested that I should use some of my old contacts and go back into the furniture and carpet retail world.

"Let's face it, Lou," she remarked. "You can sell snow to the Eskimos!" And, I can honestly say – immodest as it may seem – she was right. I probably could!

My contacts proved to be beneficial and in 1997 I started working for the insurance claims department attached to a national furniture company. My job was to call at customers' houses and inspect and verify any damage and then proceed onto a sale. Not a problem, I thought. This was something I had been doing in my own business for years. At first it was just the Tyne-Tees area but when they opened a branch in Edinburgh, Scotland, I quickly volunteered my services for the odd weekend. Here was a chance to earn some much needed extra money!

It was during one of these weekend trips in the summer of 1998 that I had a house call to the Inverness-shire village of Beauly and it was here I met someone new, my soon to be, second wife. So when the opportunity arose for me to take a full-time position there, I took it, leaving my life in Newcastle behind. A difficult decision, one would have asked? And normally I would agree, but for some inexplicable reason, it felt right.

Throughout my life – like stepping stones – circumstances had brought its own consequences that had led me to this new road. A road that – unknown to myself at the time – would completely change my whole way of thinking and answer questions that I had been asking myself through the years.

Maybe this was my destiny? In the past I hadn't really believed in all of that 'fate' stuff, but maybe I had been wrong.

Maybe this was something that had been planned; my purpose in life? Something that had been destined for me from being a small child from the back streets of Tyneside into making me what I am today.

This is my incredible journey in search of 'The Truth'.

CHAPTER ONE (part one)
PRELUDE OF A SECRET DYNASTY:
THE SECRET MISSION OF
MONTSÉGUR

Chronicled in the mists of medieval history, the Cathars of Languedoc, in southern France, played a vital role in the legends of Christianity. Despite being unfairly condemned by the Roman Catholic Church for their so-called unchristian behaviour and branded as heretics for their non-conformist beliefs, they were staunch supporters of an enigma that would be carried down for aeons to come. They were devout followers of the Mary Magdalene Dynasty.

In religious terms they were deeply spiritual people, preaching outdoors rather than in the richly ornate churches of the Catholic religion. Men, women and children were all equal. Ascetic, saintly and pacific; they lived a simple life. The Catholic Church with its rules, artefacts and trappings were irrelevant to them – they had much more awesome possessions: ones that filled the Pope and his followers with dread. The Cathars were believed to hold a secret that would shake the whole foundation of the Catholic religion forever. They were the guardians of mysterious and sacred relics. Because of their loyalty to Mary Magdalene and her bloodline, this treasure was entrusted to them for safe keeping by an order of crusading knights who had discovered this 'big secret' whilst excavating beneath the ground of the original Temple of Solomon in the Holy Land. This mysterious treasure - sought after so much by the Catholic church – was valued far beyond any material wealth and was now reputed to be hidden beneath a castle in Languedoc; the Chateau de Montségur.

Situated on top of a high, craggy tor and built in limestone in the unusual shape of an arrowhead, the castle was surrounded by a region laced with deep caves and underground rivers. This magnificent fortress was the heart of Catharism.

In the year 1209, Pope Innocent III – encouraged by the French king, Philippe II of France – sponsored the onset of the Albigensian Crusade. To him, the Cathars were an insult to Christianity and he was determined to eradicate these followers of this breakaway religion once and for all. He insisted that each and everyone be executed. By fire or the sword – it did not matter.

"How will we know who is who?" a leading knight, was bold enough to ask.

Arnaud Amaury, the head of the order of Cistercian monks and appointed Papal Legate by Pope Innocent to investigate Catharism in Languedoc, was most notable for giving the infamous and nefarious reply. A reply that would be practised by despots and dictators in far distant conflicts to come…

"Kill them all – for God knows his own!"

Men, women, children and babies; it was of no consequence. Not one was shown any mercy. Thousands – in genocidal proportions – were brutally slaughtered and the news of the destruction of innocent people and their townships sent shock waves surging throughout the nation. The invading northern army wiped out all major towns and castles, leaving a trail of massacre and injustice in their wake.

It was in the year of 1243 and the Albigensian Crusade was nearing the end. It had been bloody, ruthless and long. Now all that was left of any significance was the majestic citadel of Montségur.

For ten months the castle was under siege from the northern invaders. The peace-loving occupants withstood repeated assaults with extreme valour and fortitude, retaining the stronghold with a tenacious defiance. But, greatly outnumbered by their enemy, the subsequent fall of the mighty fortress was only a short while away. It finally capitulated to its besiegers in the January of 1244.

For three months the Cathars and their families were held as hostages within the castle walls and any attempts to break free would be met with instant death. They now had a big problem…

…It was in the darkness of night, March 16th 1244, that four Cathar advocates and a guide made a dangerous and daring escape. However, this was not to save themselves; they were on a mission. Their aim was to take away the 'treasure' of Montségur. This was not the usual booty of gold and silver; this was something much more precious. The biggest prize of all! This was something that would be capable of turning the whole of Christianity on its head in the centuries to come. Countless books and manuscripts would be written; historians would be baffled and intrigued and men would seek and chase its whereabouts throughout the globe. In the far distant future, the mere mention of its name would court controversy and debate; doubts would be instilled into enquiring minds of many people about the authenticity of the 'Greatest story ever told'.

So it was –without any question – that this treasure was priceless. The 'treasure' that the Cathars had guarded for so long was – allegedly – none other than the relics connected to the line of Jesus Christ...

The Holy Grail.

It was a long and perilous task but having succeeded in securing the objects of their assignment from a cave beneath the castle, they slipped through the besiegers' lines and made a hasty escape to the secret underground caves and rivers that honeycombed the surrounding area. They now had to plan the second stage of their mission. This time it would be a clandestine rendezvous with a long-standing ally; someone who had entrusted this treasure to them years before – the original keepers of the Grail...

CHAPTER ONE (part two)
PRELUDE OF A SECRET DYNASTY:
THE EXODUS FROM PARIS

The Knights of the Order of the Temple of Solomon, or the Knights Templar as they were later known, were the alleged keepers of the Holy Grail and other sacred relics. In the year of 1244 they were now based in northern France.

Noted as fiercely zealous and self-disciplined, these romantically-portrayed, mystic knights, clothed in a white mantle with a red cross emblazoned across the front, had made a notorious legacy for themselves of great achievement and discovery during their crucial role in the Holy Crusades. Renowned bankers of the day, they had accrued extensive power and wealth and by lending vast sums of money to every impoverished king in Europe, they became the power behind the thrones.

Although reputed to possess a haughty and cavalier arrogance, they were famed for being the most devout and trusty knights of the Crusades. They also championed another cause. They were renowned as the trail-blazers for supporting the Jesus Christ and Magdalene Dynasty. Despite animosity from the Pope and his Catholic army they still insisted on defending the good name of Mary Magdalene, staying faithful and true to her memory regardless of any impending danger that could fall upon themselves. It was also their responsibility for the safe-keeping of the mysterious, sacred relics they had secured from the Holy Temple in Jerusalem, so the Cathars knew that by returning this coveted 'treasure' back to the Templars, it was now back in safe hands.

***

It was in the year 1307 that the security of the Grail and other holy relics was once more in jeopardy. Jacques de Molay was the twenty-third and final Grand Master of the Knights Templar – a position that held both power and prestige – when the Order was dissolved by Pope Clement V after much persuasion from the King of France, Philippe 1V. Deeply in debt to the Templars, it was obvious that Philippe's action was motivated by greed. France was virtually on the verge of bankruptcy so by crushing the Order, this would not only rid himself of his debt he could also seize the Order's great wealth and mysterious sacred relics. Philippe used feeble grievances against them to disband the group. False charges were trumped up against Jacques for heinous crimes he and his fellow Templars had not committed and a warrant went out for his capture. Realising that his arrest was imminent, he now had to act swiftly.

It was under the cover of darkness on Thursday the 12th October – the eve before Jacques de Molay's arrest – when a secret exodus of three straw-covered wagons and fifty horses left the yard of the Paris Temple. Hidden underneath the straw lay chests, all containing the entire Templar treasure. It was imperative that this crucial operation was carried out with absolute stealth, speed and precision. Nothing could be left to chance. There was too much to lose. Fronted and accompanied by Gerard de Villiers and Hugues De Chalons – preceptors of the Temple and France, heavily disguised Templars steered the carts with great care as they trundled slowly away from the city.

Once clear of the outskirts of Paris and with the help of the extra horses, they headed swiftly towards the north coast of France. However, pre-warned days prior to Jacques de Molay's imminent arrest and with the same plan in mind, the Order's mighty armada of three-mast sailing ships set sail from the Templars' home port of La Rochelle to an unknown destination in northern France. History now purports that when the runaway procession that had left the Paris Temple the night before, finally reached the prescribed port, the fleet were ready waiting.

Time was now the essence as the knights quickly loaded their cargo onboard, hidden beneath the ships' holds. They had no time to spare – there was a rising midnight tide and they knew that it would not be long before the King's army would realise that the Temple's treasury was empty and would be in hot pursuit. Much to the Templars' relief when the French soldiers did arrive at La Rochelle, it was too late. Their ships had all long gone – never to be seen again.

Now the Templars had to sail to a land far enough away from their enemies. This land had to be proven to have strong and loyal connections to their cause and safe enough to leave their precious cargo until another, much more secure and permanent place could be found. But they knew that finding this place would take time, accuracy and secrecy; it would not be an easy task. They would have to build a safe haven for the relics with the help of a map devised by using their own esoteric cartography. So, in the meantime they would have to leave them with faithful allies until this more secure place could be found.

Making the decision to sail part of the fleet to the remote northern part of Britain was an easy one. Self-crowned king, Robert the Bruce, was embroiled here in a rebellion against Edward 1 of England and had recently been excluded from the Roman Catholic Church for committing a murder on holy ground. In the eyes of the church, it was not so much the murder that had brought about his exclusion but the place where the crime had been committed. That was classed as sacrilege and the Pope had no choice but to excommunicate him. This break from the confining regime of the Catholic Church with its laws and regulations, suited the knights' needs for the safe keeping of their cargo down to the ground. However, there was a much more important reason for choosing this land as their destination. Living here was a notable family with a long-standing history linking them closely with the Templars…

…Records state that since 1128 AD the Templars' most specific and loyal ally in Scotland were the St. Clairs of Caithness and Rosslyn and none so much as the present earl of the time, Henry Sinclair the seventh Baron of Rosslyn, himself – according to popular belief – a Knights Templar. The St. Clairs were also traditionally known as custodians of holy relics. So bearing these facts in mind, it was without any doubt, where they had to go. Scotland. It was the ideal haven for their 'treasure'. It was one of the few places where the Pope could not reach them.

Reputedly, their first port of call was to Leith, just outside of Edinburgh on the Firth of Forth and then on to the small Midlothian villages of Temple and Rosslyn…

CHAPTER TWO
ROSSLYN

At the time, I didn't really understand what first pulled me to Rosslyn. Maybe it was one of the articles I had read during convalescing from a health scare that had stirred up a curiosity in me that I couldn't explain.

It was in the early part of the year 2000, when – without any warning – the searing pain that shot across my chest stopped me in my tracks: completely taking my breath away. Hospital tests diagnosed and confirmed my fears. Like my mother and ancestors before me I had acute angina and being a smoker for over forty years certainly hadn't helped the condition.

The hospital consultant put it to me quite bluntly. "If you don't want another attack," he said, grimly, "you are going to have to change your lifestyle dramatically. Because, if you don't, you might not be so lucky next time."

The doctor's words became my 'wake-up call'. I wasn't ready to throw in the towel just yet. I needed to get better and get back to work. So out went the unhealthy diet and the cigarettes and in came a much more healthy regime and several boxes of pills!

During the weeks that followed, as I slowly regained my strength and confidence, I spent a lot of my spare time reading books; most of them about Scotland and its colourful history.

Seeped in legend and tradition, here is a land that has had its fair share of bloody battles and murderous feuds; plotting and intrigue – all of these playing a major role against a backdrop of rugged, windswept heights rolling down to lush, pine-forested glens and dark, lonely lochs. It is a scene that has inspired artists, poets and writers – past and present. A grand and savage beauty – and one that most Scots are proud of! Scotland's urban and rural countryside also houses many ancient castles and fascinating churches, each of them carrying their own story or legend. But it was one church in particular that caught my attention. It was an article in one of my books that drew me to it more than any of the others. Over the weeks, I kept going back to it, not once or twice – but over and over again. It was a story about a mysterious order of medieval knights and their connection with a chapel just seven miles south of Edinburgh…

***

Built by the famous Scottish family, the Sinclairs in the mid 15th century and over a hundred years after the castle itself, Rosslyn Chapel is reputed for its links with the Order of The Knights Templar. Based on sacred geometry used extensively by the Templars, Rosslyn

Chapel's architectural layout bears an uncanny resemblance to the Temple of Solomon...

Whilst in the Holy Land these crusading knights built their headquarters on the Temple Mount at the site of the original temple. It is reputed that whilst excavating beneath the ruins, the Templars discovered and took charge of a 'big secret'...

Rosslyn Chapel is filled with inscriptions and mysterious, symbolic carvings, many relating to this Holy Temple and the Knights Templars themselves. Built as a Chapel of the Holy Grail, it is here that several knights of the order including William Sinclair, the eleventh Baron of Rosslyn – himself an alleged Templar – are buried in its vaults. Legend also purports that some of the Holy relics and possibly even the Holy Grail – once guarded so passionately by the Templars, have at some time – if not still – been hidden within its walls...

***

It was a warm sunny day in mid May when I first visited Rosslyn. I had fully recovered from my illness and had returned back to my place of work in Edinburgh and was now staying at a family-run hotel on the outskirts of the city. This was in the port of Leith.

On entering the main door, I made my way to the tearoom and gift shop, briefly stopping to look at a few of the keepsakes on display. After purchasing a visitor's guide book, I entered the main chapel itself. As I quickly looked around, my first impression was one of surprise. The eerie silence, mixed with some sort of spiritual tranquillity was not what I was expecting. I immediately felt safe and at peace. I also noticed that the place was empty. Let it be said, these were the days before the 'hype' of Dan Brown's *Da Vinci Code* and the chapel was not as famous then as it is today.

Walking across the floor towards a stand holding church candles, I paused for a moment before picking one up. I knew I had to thank God for keeping me safe during the weeks I had felt so ill and – for whatever obscure reason – bringing me to this place. All of a sudden, as I watched the flickering flame, I instinctively realised that from this moment my life would never be the same again. I felt different: remote; spaced-out. It was as though I now had to focus on a new pathway in my life. My morals and principles would stay unchanged but the whole core of my being would now be centred on an ancient enigma that had tormented historians and theologians for centuries before – the mystery surrounding the Holy Grail.

I turned away from the candles and carried on looking around. I was filled with admiration and awe. Every square foot was richly decorated with symbolic and mysterious carvings etched into the stone pillars, walls and ceiling; each of them telling their own story. Characters from the Bible sit side by side with pagan, Masonic and religious images. The birth of Christ is surrounded by statues of angels, paying homage to their young king. Balanced against the seven virtues are the seven deadly sins – good versus evil– and the Devil scowls with anger as a young couple turn away from him and look across to the window of the Angel of Mercy as though seeking guidance and help. All types of trees, plants and flowers are in an abundance. Engravings of sweet corn and maize mix with cacti and sunflowers… fifty years before they were discovered by Columbus. Lilies, daisies and roses decorate the roof in a most intricate pattern. As I progressed down the chapel, I realized what a beautiful place this was… the detail; the exquisite craftsmanship; the imagination and extravagance. It was everywhere! It had to be seen to be believed.

I was now approaching the much documented Apprentice Pillar, stopping at regular intervals to admire the stunning stained-glass windows. It was the window next to the pillar depicting St James and St Jude together that caught my eye. I looked up for a moment, taking in the colours made more vibrant because of the shaft of sunlight streaming through the panes. It was then I was aware of somebody standing behind my right shoulder; obviously as interested as I was in the window and needing a closer view. I politely stepped to one side at the same time turning to see who had joined me. Every hair stood up on the back of my neck and a strange eerie feeling washed over my body. There was someone there; I was convinced of that, but I was standing alone!

Quickly moving away from the window, I drew in a deep, steadying breath; willing commonsense to rule over an increasing panic. I needed to regain my usual steady composure. I needed a distraction.

I turned and focused my attention to the legendary Apprentice Pillar. Concentration was now difficult but fortunately I already had some knowledge of this unusual but beautiful carving from reading its story during my convalescence. Legend claims that the master mason having received an order to model a pillar of exquisite design and artistry from one in Rome, hesitated to begin his work until he had visited the original to glean inspiration. During his absence, his apprentice, having dreamt of the finished pillar set to work at once and using his vision as an example, subsequently created a perfect masterpiece. When his master returned he was so incensed with jealousy he flew into a rage and picking up his mallet, he struck his apprentice on the head, killing him instantly. The mason paid for his crime of passion with his life.

Not far from the pillar I noticed an entrance to a flight of worn-down, stone stairs. A brief consultation with the guide book told me it lead to the outer crypt or sacristy. Dating back to the early 12th century and used as a place of worship, this was all that was left from the original castle before it was destroyed. It also housed the inaccessible and mysterious inner vaults supposedly containing tombs of knights lying in guard of the sacred relics that Rosslyn was noted for.

My interest kicked up a notch. This I had to see. It was as though I knew. A sort of 'déjà vu' experience. It was because of this that I descended the stairs to the sacristy with a slight trepidation. Immediately, I realised how cold the atmosphere had become. So cold – like on a winter's day – I could see my breath before me.

As I wandered about the crypt I noted several stones and tomb covers all bearing a coat-of-arms and cryptic inscriptions and crosses. At the far end of the crypt stood a grey, oblong stone with a small crucifix standing on the top. A large cross of an unusual design was displayed on the front. I took this to be a small altar of some kind. But it was the stained-glass window directly above the altar depicting the transfiguration of Christ as he ascends into heaven that caught my attention the most. It was amazing in its colour and design. As I admired its beauty, a light-headed sensation crept over my body – once more taking me by surprise. It was a weird feeling; not dissimilar to what had happened before in the chapel above, but this time it was more powerful; more intense. Rising and falling as the waves of faintness surged and ebbed it also brought with it a confusingly mixed emotion of peace and sadness. I no longer felt cold; in fact my whole body felt on fire. I definitely need some fresh air! I knew I would have to leave, so promising myself I would return at a later date, I rather reluctantly made a hasty exit.

The gardens of Rosslyn Chapel are secluded by a high stone wall and trees. Apart from the sound of birdsong coming from the trees, there was no other noise. Coupled with this and the early summer sunshine, this was a truly tranquil place. I was now feeling much better and as I walked around the lawned area taking in the stately building before me, I tried to make sense of what had just happened.

Maybe you are still feeling weak from your illness, my sensible head informed me… maybe you aren't as strong as you thought you were. Perhaps, I inwardly agreed – but my 'other' head, the impractical one – the one that had possibly drawn me here in the first place; the one that had previously been overruled so many times in my life, was now telling me otherwise. There was something special about this amazing place and I needed to know more; the history and the legend and – more importantly – these mysterious Knights Templar that seem to have so much influence here.

Sitting down on a garden bench that was on the edge of a wide, gravelled area near to grass, I opened up my guide book once more. There might be some more information here, I said to myself as I turned the pages.

It was the squeak of an un-oiled wheel or wheels and crunching on the gravel that made me look up. Squinting against the bright sunlight, I could see a tall, dark-haired, young man, possibly in his late twenties and pushing a dilapidated, old wheelbarrow coming towards where I was sitting. He stopped in front of me and nodded. Judging by the T-shirt and jeans that he was wearing and what looked like a pile of weeds in his barrow, I automatically presumed that he was a gardener.

"Hello there," he smiled, putting the barrow down at the same time. "It's lovely day, isn't it?" His Scottish accent was soft rather than strong.

On closer inspection I realised that I had more than likely miscalculated his age. The faint lines on his slightly weathered face belied his athletic physique. Probably early forties – give or take a few years – I said to myself.

"Yes, it is," I replied, returning his smile.

He looked rather hot and immediately verified my thoughts by taking out a red handkerchief from his jeans pocket and mopped his brow with it.

"It's a nice place," I commented, nodding my head in the direction of the chapel.

"Oh, aye," he agreed, at the same time as he sat down next to me. He then turned and directed his gaze straight at me as he continued to speak. "It's *more* than 'nice', mind! It's a 'one-off' as far as I am concerned, I'm afraid."

I looked at this man's face with interest. The long straight nose; the square jaw line; the vivid blue eyes – all seemed uncannily familiar somehow. An uneasy thought suddenly hit me. What the hell was going on here? Why was I looking at a fellow man so intently? This was not something I normally went round doing… in fact; to be totally honest… I couldn't remember *ever* doing! But there was just something about him that puzzled me. It was one of those faces I knew I had seen before, but – for the life of me – couldn't place it.

"Mind you, I'm going to say that, aren't I?" He carried on, "You see, I've been connected to it for long time; years in fact. It's quite important to me. *And...*" he added, emphasising the word 'and', "I know enough about it to fill a text book, so maybe I'm just a wee bit biased. You see my family have been around the family that own it for centuries." He paused and then asked, "Have *you* been inside yet?"

I nodded. "Yes, I have but I should have stayed a bit longer. You see, I misjudged the time and it wasn't until I came out that I realized. I wish I had now as there is so much more I need to know. I'm definitely going back, though." I didn't mention the real reason for leaving: the weird feelings of faintness. He didn't need to know that.

He gave me a curious look as though he didn't quite believe me, but never spoke.

"It's not so much the chapel," I carried on as I watched his gaze turn back to the chapel. "Yes, I know it is a beautiful place and well worth some more visits, but it's more about these Knights Templar and their history. That is what has got me intrigued, more than anything. I seem to be drawn to them somehow. I would love to find out more about them. They sound fascinating."

He quickly turned to look at me again and narrowed his eyes. He seemed to reflect for a few moments before replying. "R-really?" he said, slowly. "Are you sure?"

"Yes, definitely. I've been wanting to know about them for a while now. To find out…" I trailed off, not quite sure what to say next.

He pursed his lips, thought again and then nodded his head before giving me a small smile. "Okay," he said. "Well – if that is the case, maybe I can help you a bit. There isn't anything I don't know about the Templars and I'm due a break."

I looked at him with added interest. This was something I wasn't expecting. "Well that would be great. That's if you don't mind?"

He gave a short laugh. "Mind?" he echoed. "Of *course* I don't mind! As I said before my family has had connections with the owners of Rosslyn, the St. Clairs – for generations."

"St. Clair – is this their real name?" I asked. "I know they go by the name, Sinclair, now don't they?"

"Aye, they do. St. Clair or Sinclair – it doesn't matter. They were once one of the most powerful families in Scotland, you know. They came over from France with William the Conqueror in 1066."

"Oh – so they are originally from France then?"

"Aye," he replied. "They were Normans; same as my family. Mind you, we never came to Scotland until early fourteenth century. It was the St Clairs that built this place." He indicated his head towards the chapel.

"William St Clair – the eleventh baron – it was he who laid the foundations in 1446. Mind you the crypt goes back further than that. Unfortunately he died before it was finished. He was said to have modelled it on the layout of Solomon's Temple in Jerusalem…"

I remembered reading about this. "I know this," I interjected. "I've read about it in a book I bought a few weeks ago. Weren't the Templars the keepers of the keys to this Temple? And didn't they have in their possession some sort of sacred treasure?"

The gardener gave a small nod and smiled in agreement. "Aye, they were. That's how they got their name. They fought in the Christian Crusades against the Saracens and used the site of the old temple as their headquarters and it is said that while they were excavating there they found this treasure that you are going on about."

I looked at him with curiosity for a moment and then carried on. "And this so-called treasure – could this be the Holy Grail?"

He glanced at me sharply, a slight frown crossing his brow, and then looked towards the chapel as though in thought. I put this wariness down to my forthright question and I didn't want to push him. I didn't have to.

Suddenly, he turned his gaze back to look me straight in the face and gave a bright smile.

"So the story goes." His reply was short and non-informative. It was as though he was waiting for me to continue.

"So what happened to it next?" I asked.

"Well, they took it to a castle in the south of France first and there it stayed until it was raided by the Catholic army in 1244. The castle belonged to a group of people called the Cathars, loyal allies to the Templars. They were peaceful, simple folk with simple ideas but the Catholics were against their non-conformist beliefs."

"What were they?"

"Well, they were unorthodox pacifists who believed that men and women were equal," he explained. "They didn't believe in churches and would pray and preach in the open air. They opposed the rules and regulations of the Catholic Church conforming only to their own beliefs. They also believed in the sanctity and the truth behind the holy relics and what they could mean to mankind. So the Pope ordered them to be destroyed: their towns; villages; castles and people. 'Kill them all' was the instruction to the soldiers – men, women, children; everybody —"

"Nice," I cut in, sarcastically.

"Quite!" He smiled ironically, nodding at the same time before continuing, "So, just before the castle was taken, the Cathars managed to smuggle the secret treasure out and it was finally brought to the Templars' headquarters in Paris. It stayed there for many years – well, until 1307 to be exact – this is when the French king along with the Pope's blessing, wanted the order of the Knights Templar dissolved.

I looked puzzled. "I don't quite understand here," I frowned. "If they were good, Christian knights why would they want to do this?"

The gardener took in a deep breath. "Well, first of all – they *were* good knights. They were classed as the Warriors of Christ and originally employed by the Pope. But, let's not forget that what they had in their possession was something so powerful it could shake the Catholic Church to its very core. Remove all its credibility. So, there was *no* way the church wanted this to come out – *ever*. They would do *anything* to stop that."

"So, what is this big secret you are talking about?" I asked, completely intrigued by it all. "It's all to do with the Holy Grail, isn't it?" My words were a direct statement rather than a question. I knew the answer, but I needed to hear it confirmed from this stranger's mouth.

He looked at me as though he was trying to weigh me up for a few seconds and then made a decision.

"M'mm," he said finally with a wry smile. "Well, it depends what you class as the 'Holy Grail'; there are many theories on this. So, I'll let *you* make your own mind up on that one."

"Okay." I nodded slowly, making a quick mental note that I would do this whilst at the same time realising that here was a 'cop-out' if ever there was one!

Right," he continued, his voice taking on a more serious tone. "You see, there is a much more important aspect to all of this. Because, what I am going to tell you next is not what is generally accepted by the church – be it Catholic; Protestant; Methodist or whatever… it doesn't matter. We are talking about a lot of Christians everywhere —" Another short pause.

I sat forward on my seat in anticipation. This was like something out of a Hollywood adventure movie. Only instead of being fiction – it was real life!

"R-right?" I asked, expectantly.

"Right!" he reiterated, firmly. "Okay then… as you likely know, it is written in the New Testament that Christ died on the cross and on the third day He ascended into heaven. Well, the Templars didn't believe it happened like that. They believe it was a case of resuscitation rather than resurrection. It happened in those days, trust me. You see, they believed that Jesus was a man; a very good man; a holy man, in fact – *but* – a 'man', all the same. Someone who lived with a man's emotions and needs. And someone – no matter where *or* when he died – whose remains would be here on earth."

"I always thought there was something about the crucifixion that wasn't quite right," I informed him, hurriedly. "I felt we were never given the whole story."

"Well *you* are right," he confirmed, emphatically. "And the Templars made no secret of this belief, which is why the Catholic Church disagreed with this so-called blasphemy and declared them as heretics. They needed Jesus Christ to ascend into heaven like the scriptures say and – in those days – to question this was a terrible crime. *But* – there something else they believed in; something that really shook the whole foundation of the church and that was Mary Magdalene —"

"She was the prostitute that Jesus saved, wasn't she?" I interjected.

A deep scowl immediately darkened his face and I took in a short, silent breath. Strange as it was, my remark seemed to have angered him and that was the last thing I wanted to do. I had so many more questions waiting for answers.

"*No!*" he asserted strongly, his voice rising slightly. "She was *no* prostitute – reformed or otherwise! She was Jesus' wife and mother of his children —."

"Children!? – there *are* children?" I interrupted again, lowering my voice as though there were eavesdroppers about listening into our conversation when in fact there was nobody else around.

The scowl disappeared as quickly as it had appeared, but I could feel it was still a sore subject with him.

"Aye, there were," came his rather gruff reply. "Three. The youngest – a boy – is rumoured to have settled here in Scotland."

"Is there proof of this?" I asked; once more the 'Doubting Thomas' was riding in.

"Aye, there is." He sounded sure about this: his tone much softer now. "But you will have to look into that one. The information is all out there."

"R-right, I will," I said slowly, making another mental memo to myself and then pondered on this for a moment before speaking. "So, if this is the case," I then added, thoughtfully. "There could be descendants of Christ walking around, then?"

"Of course there is," he affirmed strongly with a trace of rancour in his voice. "That is what the church couldn't accept. The bloodline of Christ and Mary Magdalene. In their eyes this was and still is – unacceptable. They wanted to keep the story of the 'resurrection' of this man as pure and holy. In those days *they* wanted to keep the power in the church and not have some dynasty out there threatening this. So they needed a man not capable of physical love for a woman – sins of the flesh – so to speak. And if you can recall, the gospels write that Mary was the only disciple that he kissed on the mouth. That was something unheard of in those days unless of course she was his wife. So they had to explain her constant presence in his life —."

I nodded, thoughtfully. "So they made her into something she wasn't!"

His eyes clouded over. "Aye, they did just that!" he said with disdain. "They made her into a whore!"

Now, for some reason, beyond any logic that I could understand, I joined in with his anger and sat up stiffly. "So really," I declared. "There is a bloody massive miscarriage of justice here that has been carried on for centuries! It's terrible! The poor woman!" I sounded annoyed; I couldn't help it.

He looked at me closely with a slightly, concerned frown. "Aye, you're right, it is," he agreed, sadly. And then seemingly aware of my annoyance, he quickly returned to his story of the Grail. "Now, I seem to have digressed a wee bit here," he continued. "Where was I? Ah – yes, 1307 and the order is about to be dissolved."

He sounded and looked much happier again. I had noticed how very quickly his moods changed and I surmised from this he could be of a fiery disposition.

Not one to be crossed with, I mused to myself. Probably the French blood!

"You see," he carried on. "I don't know whether you know or not, but the Templars were the bankers of their day. It was they who introduced the banking institution – with the cheques and interest on loans. It's through them that we have the banks that we have today."

"Yes," I replied with a nod. "I do know a bit about this, but tell me more."

"Well," he obliged with a small smile. "By lending money to many destitute kings in Europe, they became the power behind the thrones and accrued a great wealth. Philippe 1V of France was not happy about this and thought if he could get the Pope's permission he could get the order disbanded. This meant his debt would be wiped out and then he could get his hands on the Templars' vast fortune. He trumped up some terrible charges against them – blasphemy, sodomy – even to perverse behaviour with animals. Jacques de Molay, the Grand Master of the Templars was tortured into falsely confessing and they tried to crucify him. But he somehow survived this and when he later retracted his statement to say it been exacted under torture, Philippe still sent an order out for his death. This time for heresy. He was burnt at the stake on an island on the River Seine March 1314 – seven years later."

"A great man, then!" I remarked.

"A great man all right!" he returned, with earnest. "He bore his pain with courage and dignity, proudly denying any of the crimes of which he and the Templars had been accused, right up to the very end. He was a very much admired and respected man." The gardener's feelings on this legendary man were obvious by the tone of admiration in his voice.

"His legacy still goes on today, doesn't it?" I remarked, remembering what I had read about this famous knight.

He nodded in total agreement. "Yes, definitely," he replied. "It has incited other similar organizations through the years. They have all been inspired by Jacques de Molay." He paused as though in sad reflection for a moment.

I looked at him with some concern. He seemed distracted by what he just told me: distant; upset even. I needed him to carry on with his story.

"So after Jacques' arrest, what happened to their treasure?" I asked, quietly.

"Well, they had to do something and quickly," he replied, swiftly regaining his composure. "They didn't have much time. Keeping it safe was crucial to the Templars. They smuggled it out of Paris onto their many sailing ships. Many of the lucky knights sailed with them but *many* also died in France along with Jacques."

"Is this when they brought it to Scotland?" I asked him.

"Some of it – yes, definitely. There is so much evidence to support this, especially here at Rosslyn. Mind you, they didn't come straight here. They made their way to the village of Ballantrodoch first —."

"Ballantro... doch?" I sounded puzzled. The name definitely rang a bell, but I wasn't quite sure.

"Aye," he nodded. "It's just down the road. You probably know it best as Temple."

I nodded in acknowledgement. "Ah, yes, I know where you mean now."

"Well, this was where their headquarters were. You see, it was in 1126 that King David the first of Scotland granted the Templars' land there in recognition for their works in the Crusades. It was here that the first Templar preceptory was built outside the Holy Land and this is where they stayed. It wasn't until much later in 1618, that the name was changed, though."

"That's interesting," I said. "But when did the connection of Rosslyn begin?"

"The St. Clairs who owned the land at Rosslyn had a close association with the Templars. They were their trusted friends from the crusades. Their connection with each other goes without saying." He then pointed his finger in the direction of the chapel. "Take the chapel for instance; you have only got to look around and you'll see for yourself. Their crosses, for instance. They are the ones with the four or eight points and, of course – there's the grailed and splayed crosses themselves. And then there's their symbols and markings – they are everywhere in there!"

"Oh," I said. "I never noticed."

He then stood up and looked down at me, a hint of a playful smile curving his mouth. "Because *you* are one of the uninitiated," he pointed out with just a touch of mock rebuke in his voice. "You see, you *have* to know what you are looking for!"

"Right!" I responded, standing up to join him. I had realised he was about to take his leave and I didn't even know his name. "By the way, I'm sorry, but I don't know your name."

"That's because you never asked," came the dry reply. "Anyway – now you have, it's John. And yours?"

"It's Lou," I replied. "Lou Jones."

"And that's short for Louis?" He sounded sure of his assumption. "Not Lewis? Am I right?"

I gave a short laugh and nodded. "Yes, you are right!" I replied, sounding slightly bemused. "Well, anyway, thanks John, for your time. It's been interesting talking to you. I'm definitely coming back for another look around, so maybe we will meet again someday?"

"Maybe." He grinned as he picked up his wheelbarrow. "Well, Lou, I had best be off – work to be done and all that! Take care of yourself, won't you?"

"You too."

As I watched him walk back from where he came from, I felt a slight tinge of sadness. Even though I had only met this stranger a very short while ago, I was sorry to see him go. Seemingly moody and somewhat arrogant he might have been, but – for a strange reason – I seemed to have formed some sort of affinity with him. I had to sit back down in order to recollect my confused thoughts. I felt sad and assertive at the same time. I could now understand why these Knights Templar had defied the Catholic Church. Why they had guarded their sacred relics so fiercely and for so long. And last – but certainly not least – why they had such a strong devotion and loyalty to one of the most misjudged women in traditional history... Mary Magdalene.

What little information I had known previously about these magnetic knights, was no longer enough. I had to know more. I now had a great empathy towards them and everything they had stood for. I felt as though a great burden had been placed upon my shoulders, but at the same time another burden – the one of self-doubt, disillusionment and wondering – had been lifted. It was a weird emotion. And, it was one that was going to take over my life – not for a few weeks or months – but for a long time to come and at this present moment in time, I wasn't quite sure the reason why.

CHAPTER THREE
QUEST FOR THE TRUTH

After my visit to Rosslyn Chapel most of my spare time was spent trawling new and second-hand bookshops gathering as much information as I could about the Knights Templar and everything connected to them. Ever since my meeting with the gardener with his tales of mystery, murder and sacred treasure, my thoughts rarely stopped recalling what he had told me. It was as though he had planted the seeds of knowledge and now I had to allow them to grow. It was like being given just the first few chapters of a best-selling novel and not having the rest of the story and now it was up to me to fill in the blank pages. But this was no novel; unlike fiction, this had to be fact. I could only relate it to being like one very long history lesson and I was my own tutor.

My reading material became my new pastime and I became the biggest bookworm around! It was all out there... The holy crusades; the peace loving and abused Cathars; the demise of the Templars' Order followed by the brutal and unjust death of their beloved leader – Jacques de Molay; both of these deeds solicited by greedy and cruel French kings and misguided Popes.

And then came the knights' secret naval escape from Northern France to distant lands in a frantic mission to save their precious cargo and finally, the arrival of their sailing ships onto the shores of Scotland. These medieval knights – bold, enigmatic and charismatic and notorious for their passionate belief in the Magdalene Dynasty – are most certainly what historical legends are made of! I was hooked! The more I read the more I wanted to know. I was like a man on a mission; I had to know it all! I now knew I had a job to do and subconsciously, I was being led down a path – destination unknown.

***

It was three months from my first visit that I returned to Rosslyn Chapel. After my last rather swift exit, I had promised myself I would go back and also I wanted to find these symbols, carvings and crosses that John the gardener had spoken about. This time I was prepared. No more 'funny turns', I told myself sternly. This time I would be looking at the chapel in a different light. This time it would be not as a first-time tourist but as an amateur historian – so to speak! After sifting through my alarmingly, increasing pile of literature, I felt confident about the purpose of my visit. I now had a good idea what I was looking for.

***

On entering the Lady Chapel, I immediately felt the same overwhelming mix of awe and peace as I did before. This amazing place certainly had a spiritual aura about it! When this is added to the ornate and intricate design of the surrounding walls, roof and pillars – each and everyone carried out with such precision and detail; not just with beauty but with meaning too – it is plausible to say that the exquisite artistry of Rosslyn could rival any church, minster or even cathedral in the land. This time though – unlike previously – I was not looking at the craftsmanship. I was on the lookout for any recognizable Templar attributions that could validate their presence at Rosslyn. And just as I had been told... the hidden signs and seals were all there!

In the vault of each bay in the main chapel and also arching across the ceiling of the crypt below are carvings of the 'Engrailed Cross'; the central symbol of the Sinclair coat of arms. On closer inspection, the junction of these crosses – subtly, but nevertheless distinctive – is the splayed cross or 'Croix Patte' used so often by the Templars whilst fighting in the crusades.

The stone-vaulted roof of the choir bears Templar connections in abundance too. Set amid a panoramic field of five pointed stars are the moon and the sun; the cornucopia; a dove in flight offering an olive branch; all of them signs of the knights love of astrology. Etched on a small pillar on the north wall to the left of the window is an engraving in the form of 'The Agnus Dei' or the 'Lamb of God' – a symbol of the martyred Christ and used as one of the Templars' seals.

Within the chapel walls are two Templar burial tombs. Earl William Sinclair, the founder of Rosslyn, lies in the North aisle of the chapel. Carved onto the front of the stone tomb is the distinctive floriated cross and bearing within it, is the splayed Templar cross. Taking this intimate combination of symbols on the side of the burial stone into consideration, surely must confirm the Order's connection with the Sinclairs and Rosslyn?

It was now I had to recall the gardener's mild rebuke – the Templars' signs do abound throughout the chapel. "You just have to know what you are looking for!" he had informed me. And he was so right!

So, by taking his bluff advice, I had looked and found the signs and symbols everywhere, but none so much as the evident 'Engrailed Crosses'. By uniting the Sinclair Coat of Arms and the Templars' seal within this cross, is it not pertinent to suppose that the Sinclair family played not just an important role in supporting and protecting the Order after it was so cruelly suppressed in France in 1307, but also in managing to keep and preserve the memory of these Warrior Knights of Christ right up to the present day?

Unlike before, I left the chapel at a much more leisurely rate. There had been no feelings of faintness – just a pleasant, relaxed sensation; so completely opposite to my last visit. So this time a cup of coffee was definitely on the menu!

The tearoom-cum-gift shop, despite being small, was not busy – a half dozen customers at the most; so finding an empty table was easy. As I drank my coffee, I noticed that someone had left a guide-book on the table next to me. Picking it up, I began to flick through the pages and thought how much my daughter would love it here. Living in my home town of Newcastle upon Tyne, both my children now had families of their own.

Paul, my son and the youngest of the two is a man of many talents… published artist and professional photographer; aspiring musician, singer/songwriter; one-time pantomime dame and 'Elvis' impersonator plus a respectable day-job of selling executive cars are just a few of the strings he has to his bow!

Louise, the eldest, on the other hand, is a much acclaimed and sought after medium and clairvoyant. Some cynics might suggest that I am a wee bit biased here – and understandably so – but like the many people that seek her out for spiritual guidance and comfort, her gift of mediumship and foresight never ceases to amaze me! As with many other fellow psychics, anything to do with cryptic symbols and signs and mysterious and ancient legends and phenomena is right up her street! She also shares my passion for the mystery surrounding the ancient tale of the Holy Grail and – even more so – the controversial theory of the Mary Magdalene dynasty and the bloodline of Jesus Christ. She would be so enthralled with this place, I told myself. I had to buy her something as a keepsake: something for her to have until she could visit this remarkable chapel herself.

On finishing my coffee, I walked over to the gift shop at the end of the room.

"This is so unusual," the young assistant behind the counter remarked as she looked at the mystic looking, silver Celtic cross and chain I had just handed her.

"Yes, it is," I replied, handing her a twenty pound note at the same time. "It's for my daughter. I hope she likes it. I think she will as she loves anything like this." I then felt the need to explain. "You see, she's a clairvoyant, so she is into anything with a spiritual theme."

"Ooh, that's interesting," the assistant said. "I must say, I'm into all of that too. Does she do the cards?"

I nodded. "If you mean the Tarot cards – then yes, she does. But she does other things as well. Anything spiritual, really. I *know* she would love it here. It's the second time I have been and it's got a lovely air about the place."

She nodded her head and smiled. "I know exactly what you mean," she said as she placed the necklace into a small gift bag. "We have lots of visitors who come in here and say exactly the same. It *has* got a special feel about it, hasn't it?"

"It certainly has!" I agreed. "And there is so much detail in everything and not just that – it's the history, as well. When I was here in May, I met your gardener and he told me loads about it. It was absolutely fascinating!"

"We aim to please." She smiled, as she handed me the gift.

"I was hoping to see him again, if that's possible," I continued. "That's if he's here today."

"They should be." The assistant answered. "There's two of them as a rule. What was his name?"

"John," I replied. "Quite a tall man with dark hair. Possibly in his early forties."

The assistant gave a small frown. "M'mm," she said as though she was thinking. "I'm not sure about a 'John'. There is definitely an 'Alistair' but he's older than that. He was in here earlier on having a coffee, but I'm not sure about the other one, though – I think he's quite new. Hang on a minute." She looked over to an older assistant who was stacking some brochures on a nearby table. "Janet," she said, raising her voice slightly as she looked across. "What's the name of the gardener... not Alistair... the other one? It's not 'John' is it?"

The assistant – who I can now call 'Janet' turned to look at us both.

"It's Ian," she replied firmly.

"No 'John', then?" I looked and sounded puzzled.

Janet frowned and shook her head. "N-o, I don't think so," she replied, slowly. " We tend to talk to them quite a bit when they come to the tearoom and I definitely can't remember a 'John'. I've worked here for two years now, but the name doesn't ring a bell."

"He said he was a friend of the Sinclairs – his family have known them for years," I remarked, hoping this information would help.

"Oh well, if that's the case, he might not have come in here," she said. "Also they sometimes take on temporary staff, especially in the summer when it's busy."

That's probably it, I thought after thanking them for their help and making my way to exit. It was the only logical explanation…

***

It was the sound of a petrol lawnmower that drew my attention to the garden.

I had to go and look. Just in case… I thought… You never know… It could be?

An older gentleman, wearing a cream, straw trilby on his head, was pushing a large mower across the grass. I watched as he stopped at the edge of a flowerbed and began to talk to another man about the same age as himself who was tending to some plants. They became engrossed in a deep conversation with each other and then judging by the loud laughter that followed, I presumed there must have been a joke in there somewhere!

I wonder which one is 'Alistair' and which one is 'Ian'? I mused, smiling slightly. No 'John' though? Well, put it this way, it certainly doesn't look like it, my inner voice continued as the smile faded. But then was I expecting him to be here? I wasn't sure about that. This was madness – I knew that, but this mysterious stranger had certainly stirred up some sort of incentive in me that I didn't yet fully comprehend. Would we meet again?

"Maybe," had been his cryptic reply.

But as I walked away, leaving the garden and Rosslyn behind a deep instinct told me that we probably wouldn't. There was no need. Not any more. He had done his job well.

CHAPTER FOUR
THE LADY OF DIRLOT

The county of Caithness on the lonely, most northern coast of Scotland offers scenery of dramatic contrasts, from the tall, storm-swept coastal cliffs to secluded sandy bays. Small fishing boats sail in and out of the many harbours followed by hungry seabirds soaring high above; their raucous cries filling the air. Whilst inland, craggy peaks and tors roll down onto peaty bogs. Heather-clad hills surround and protect the flora and fauna filled nature reserves. It is to this county that my journey now takes an unexpected detour.

It is now the early summer of 2003 and I was still driving around the mainland and islands following up insurance claims. Visits to historic places that I had never seen before brought with them tales of heroism and hardship that I had never heard of before. From the wild and rugged beauty of the highlands to the more mellow picturesque scenery of the lowlands, I gradually became an expert on Scotland and its colourful history and – at same time – a great advertisement for the Scottish Tourist Board! New stories were added on to the 'old'. The information was endless! Tall tales of kelpies, unicorns, monsters of the deep and folklore describing magical places were in abundance everywhere – some fabulous, maybe and some – maybe not. But the legend that kept cropping up to haunt me more than all of the others, was the one of the Knights Templar and their sacred treasure. The tales of this ancient mystery and everything that surrounds it was evident all over Scotland and its islands. But it was always to Rosslyn and the knights' connection with the family of St. Clairs that my thoughts would always return.

I was now on my way to Caithness to assess four insurance claims. Having booked into a small hotel in the town of Thurso for the night, I decided to do the first three claims which were near the town centre straight away and the next day drive six miles south to a much larger property near Loch Calder. Looking at the worksheet, I could see that the name of the house was succeeded with the word 'Hall'.

Not the normal 'run-of-the-mill' type of property then, I presumed to myself! The name of the owner was a Major Charles Stuart Esquire... Very Scottish, I must say... my mind continued, drolly... I wonder if he is related to the great man himself by any chance?!

The house – or 'the big house' as the local villager called it when I stopped to ask for directions – could not be seen from the road. A private gatehouse stood next to two closed high iron gates that barred any unexpected visitors from entering. After explaining to the gatekeeper the purpose of my visit, he made a phone call and then seconds later the gates opened by a remote locking system.

As I drove up the winding, private road I couldn't help noticing that – apart from fleeting shafts of sunlight shining through the leaves – the tall trees flanking each side completely blocked out any view. It was serene and secluded; like going back in time. I was well impressed! As I turned the final bend, the large house – possibly dating back to the late eighteenth century – suddenly appeared in front of me; as though out of nowhere. The picture of this striking property sitting near the edge of the tranquil loch, made an excellent first impression to any visitor!

As I stopped the car outside the house, an elderly couple were already waiting at the main entrance.

I gave them a broad smile as I walked over and immediately introduced myself. "Hello, pleased to meet you. I'm Lou – Lou Jones," I said, shaking both their hands in turn as I spoke.

The gentleman of the house bowed his head, graciously. "Welcome, sir," he said, politely. "I'm Charles Stuart and this is my wife, Elizabeth."

I smiled and nodded in recognition to his wife. "Hello there," I said.

She immediately smiled in return. "Pleased to meet you too," she said, pleasantly. "But, come in – come in!" She then added hurriedly, ushering me through the front door.

I followed them down a long hall and then through another doorway. Considering the size of the house, the room was not as large as I expected it to be. The rather dated décor and style; with a hotchpotch collection of settees, chairs and furniture of all different coloured woods and family portraits and photographs adorning the walls and mantelpiece, was not what caught my attention the most. It was the panoramic view from a pair of French windows at far end of the room. The wide expanse of the loch with a back cloth of rich green pine trees extended right across my field of vision, filling both panes of the glass. The morning sun that reflected onto the blue-grey waters gave it a sparkling, dappled effect. It was like looking at a picture postcard. A truly splendid sight!

Elizabeth gave me another warm smile. "Would you like some refreshments?" she asked. "Tea, coffee – maybe? I'd offer you something a wee bit stronger, but you are driving, aren't you?!" Her eyes showed a playful twinkle and I wasn't quite sure whether she was teasing me or not. Also, taking into account that it was only mid-morning, I chose to believe that she was!

"Coffee would be great, thank you," I answered, once more returning her smile.

As she disappeared out of the room, the Major walked across the room to a chesterfield settee that was sitting not far from the French window. Propped up against the arm of the settee was a mahogany table. The deep crack across the top was immediately obvious.

"Well, this is it," he said, as I bent down to inspect the table. "It doesn't look good, does it?" He waited a moment before adding, "It was my son," he explained. "He was up a ladder changing a light bulb when he lost his balance and fell onto the table!"

"I hope he was okay," I remarked with a concerned frown, looking up to the high ceiling. "It's quite a long way down from there!"

"Oh, *he's* fine," the Major said airily, dismissing his son's plight with a small wave of his hand. "It's the table that came off worse. I couldn't believe it. It's a family heirloom."

It didn't take an expert to see that by the markings underneath the table that this was a valuable piece of furniture and judging by the damage it was more than likely beyond repair. I would have to make my report and then leave it to the experts to decide.

I indicated to an easy chair in front of a coffee table directly opposite the Chesterfield settee. "May I?" I asked.

"Of course, of course, " he replied, quickly.

I sat down in the chair and took the necessary paperwork out of my briefcase.

"This is a lovely view that you have here," I commented, glancing out of the window.

"We like it," he replied, sitting down on the settee facing me. "This is our favourite room of the house. Not the biggest by any means, but it's fine when there is just the two of us. We spend a lot of time in here." He then stopped speaking as though not wanting to distract me from my writing.

I had just about finished when the rattle of cups on saucers made me look up. Elizabeth, carrying a tray laden with coffee and assorted biscuits entered the room.

She placed the tray onto the coffee table and then sat down next to her husband.

"I was just telling the Major what a lovely view you have," I said to her.

"Oh, for goodness' sake!" she said, good-naturedly as she picked up a white china coffee pot and began to pour the coffee into the cups. "Call him 'Charles' – everybody else does. We don't stand on ceremony here!" She then looked up from what she was doing and smiled at me, before adding, "Do you take milk and sugar?"

"Milk and two sugars, please," I replied.

"Yes," she continued after she had handed me my cup and saucer. "You mentioned the view. It is magnificent, isn't it? Every season is different. It is so peaceful."

I accepted the coffee and sat back slightly in my chair.

"Have you lived here long?" I asked, directing the question to them both.

It was the Major who answered first. "Well," he replied. "I was born here in 1920, but I left home when I was eighteen to go to university in England just before the war began. In 1940 I joined the army. After finishing training at Sandhurst, I was deployed straight away to Malaya to fight the Japanese."

I did a quick mental calculation on his age and realised for an eighty-three-year-old he was still in pretty good shape for his advancing years!

"Did you leave the army after the war?" I asked him.

"No – no. Not at all," he said, shaking his head. "I served another twenty years after that. It was during that time I met Elizabeth." He turned and smiled at his wife with affection. "I met her whilst I was home on leave. She's a local girl, you know! From a very famous family, actually. Our two families have been close friends for years."

Elizabeth nodded in agreement and then joined in with the conversation. "That was in 1948," she said. "He was quite a dashing young man in those days, I can tell you! A proper 'ladies' man'! He finally charmed me into marrying him two years later. Our two children were born in 1951 and 1953, but we didn't move here until 1960 when Charles' father passed away. Whether our eldest son will take over one day, I don't really know–"

"I would like to think he will!" the Major interrupted, firmly. "There has always been a 'Stuart' here since it was built in 1796 – and I'd like to think there always will be!" He then turned to his wife as though for reassurance and added, "We love the old place and wouldn't live anywhere else, would we?"

"*We* wouldn't – no," she agreed. "We do love it here, but you know what the young of today are like? They class this as too old, draughty and far too big!"

"I love old buildings that have a bit of history behind them," I said. "Especially castles and churches. I went to Rosslyn Chapel, near Edinburgh not long ago. That really fascinated me."

"Rosslyn, eh?" Elizabeth said, with a small, knowing smile. "Now that's a coincidence! You see, my maiden name is Sinclair." She then paused and thought for a moment, before standing up quickly from the settee. "Ahh – I've just remembered something that might interest you. Please excuse me for a moment, I won't be long." She gave me with another small smile and then left the room.

Major Charles Stuart was an interesting and engaging old gentleman and full of 'old school' charm. He was also very proud of his Scottish clan name. He told me about how his ancestors had fought in famous Scottish battles through the centuries and right up to modern day, World War Two. He explained how he had joined the Argyll and Sutherland Highlanders as a young lieutenant, fighting in battles in Malaya, Singapore and the Mediterranean. He was twenty-two years old.

It was Elizabeth returning into the room, carrying in her hand what looked like two pamphlets that stopped our conversation.

"I am *so* sorry I have taken so long," she said, sitting back down on the settee. "But I had trouble finding the ones I had in mind."

I must admit, I had been so engrossed in the Major's tales and exploits of valour and comradeship that I had forgotten all about the time. Taking a sly peek at my watch, I could see she had been gone for nearly half an hour.

"That's okay," I told her. "Your husband has been keeping me entertained." For the life of me, I couldn't call him 'Charles'. Maybe it was my military background that brought with it a respect for commissioned officers – especially ones that were over twenty years my senior!

"Oh, I hope he hasn't been boring you!" she remarked, giving him a mock look of reproof.

"Not at all," I returned, smiling at the Major. "Quite the opposite, in fact. He's been telling me about your family history."

"That's okay then," she said. "Because I know what he is like when he gets going!" She then offered me the pamphlets. "I thought you might want to read these – they are the local newsletters. I help with the editing every month. There is a couple of stories in them you might find interesting."

I thanked her and began to flick through the pages, not sure whether I was meant to read them there and then.

"It's all right," she said, as though reading my thoughts. "You don't have to do it now. Take them with you, I don't need them back. Then you can read them at your own leisure."

Thanking her again, I slipped them into my briefcase – telling her I would definitely look at them as soon as I could.

It was much later that evening – sitting in my hotel room – that I began to read them.

The article about two castles and a 12th century church were interesting enough, but there was one particular story that kept jumping out at me more than the others. It was about a small place called Dirlot, four miles downstream from the small picturesque village of Westerdale. It was a place I felt curiously compelled to go and visit.

***

Far off the beaten track and on a secluded bend of the River Thurso, a forty-foot-high grassy precipice plummets down into a watery and rocky ravine. Here the dark and mysterious pool that washes around the base of the precipice is fabled to house on its bed – an elusive pot of gold. This is fiercely guarded by a malevolent water kelpie. On promising to show any 'would-be' treasure hunters where the gold lies, the mythical creature entices these poor misguided souls down into the water and then – reputedly – drowns them! Deep, dark and dangerous, this stretch of the river is aptly named the 'Devil's Pool'!

Reaching up from this notorious gorge is the rocky, pinnacle that was once the site of possibly the most isolated and smallest stronghold in Scotland – Dirlot castle. Built in the early 14th century it originally consisted of a three-storeyed keep with two smaller towers at its base. Now all that is left are just a few remnants of stone.

Not much to see there, then – I told myself as I read the article for the first time. However, it was the aerial picture on the same page that had caught my attention the most. This looked a lot more interesting!

Standing near the sparse remains of the castle was a walled burial ground dating back to the early 14th century. An old cemetery situated miles away from anywhere was puzzling enough, but there was something else that made it even more intriguing. Not noticed from one's eye-level on the ground but so evident from the 'bird's-eye' photograph… it was familiarly unusual in its design. It was built in the shape of an arrowhead.

Mmm, I pondered to myself as I brought back to mind my reading material from the past couple of years… now where have I seen that before!?

***

The road to Dirlot and the castle were quite well sign-posted, but unfortunately, about one mile from the site itself, the single road became a dirt-track. Okay – maybe, for a four-by-four or a similar form of transport, but it was certainly not the right terrain for my type of vehicle! I parked my car on a nearby grassy verge and following the river's course; I continued the rest of my journey by foot.

I must have walked for about three hundred yards when I reached a sharp bend in the river. It was from this point I could now see the whole picture.

The scene before me was awesome. It was exactly how it was described in the newsletter but with a serene and ethereal atmosphere. I felt as though I was in the middle of nowhere with nothing around me but blue skies, sunshine and wild and beautiful scenery. I had to stand still for a moment to fully appreciate the view. Directly opposite me and impossible not to notice was a limestone wall, behind which I presumed was the weirdly situated burial ground. And then, to the left of this – with grass-covered mounds on each side – a gigantic pinnacle of rock dropped vertically down to a deep pool of inky, dark water below: its lofty presence completely dominating the scene.

With the graveyard being so close by, this *has* to be the 'Devil's pool' – I told myself, as I clamoured up the grassy mound that ran alongside the river. Now, as I carried on walking in the direction of the graveyard, I could see tops of tombs and what looked like a stone statue of an angel visible over the wall.

The old and rusty iron gate creaked loudly as I opened it and stepped inside.

Why would anyone want to build a cemetery here? This was the first question I asked myself, as I began to look around. It didn't make sense. Apart from there being no easy access, it would have been a hell of a distance to carry the coffin! This amused me slightly as I walked across to the wall opposite the gate. The ten foot moss-covered statue sitting on the inner edge of the wall was not an angel as I first thought but a mysterious woman clothed in ancient robes. Kneeling as though in homage, with her hands crossed lovingly over her chest, she looks over her shoulder in the direction of over the wall. Somehow, she looked out of place.

I looked up at her with a puzzled frown.

"What are you doing here?" I asked out loud. "Or better still, who *are* you? You've got no wings so you're definitely not an angel. A saint of some sort, then maybe…" I paused for a few moments and began to look around her for some clues to her identity… but there was nothing. Looking back up to the statue, I continued with my odd little soliloquy. "Well I can't find anything so I'll just have to call you the Lady of Dirlot. Okay?" I paused again as though waiting for a reply and then reality quickly kicked in.

Oh, my God – my inner voice cried – I'm losing the bloody plot here! I had to be... why else would I be trying to have a conversation with a piece of stone!? I shook my head in self-disbelief and leant against the wall. Looking over, I took a sharp intake of breath. I didn't realise how high the burial ground stood from the water level. About fifty feet down – silent, black and perilous – was the Devil's Pool.

I gave a small satisfied smile. Ahh, I see – maybe that's it, I thought, looking at the statue... You are guarding the gold!

Convinced that I had now solved the puzzle of the 'Lady of Dirlot', I carried on looking around the burial ground. Amongst the ancient headstones, I could see that some carried faint, barely legible markings of what looked like bones inscribed on them. If they are, then they *are* connected to the Templars, I told myself, remembering that I had read an article about this. It came as no surprise that I wasn't surprised! Why should I be? It seemed that the memory of these knights was following me everywhere... I was getting used to it!

With one last glance at the lady, I left the graveyard and made my way up towards the nearby craggy, moss-covered pinnacle that resembled the description in the newsletter. Puzzling from a defence point of view, this was the bizarrely situated site of Dirlot Castle. Next to nothing now remains of the castle, the article had read. This I had to see. The article was right – all I could find were a few pieces of grey stone scattered around where the base of the castle once stood!

I was now starting to flag… all this walking and climbing was beginning to take its toll. I needed to get my breath back before the long hike back to my car. Looking around I noticed a large, flat, unusual shaped stone embedded in the grassy ground nearby. This stone is not native to Caithness, I puzzled. It's the wrong colour – not the colour that Caithness is famous for. Strange, I wonder how it got here? With this in mind, I precariously sat down on it and began to think.

Sitting there, bathed in warm sunshine with only the sound of birdsong and rushing water for company, I had never felt so at peace with life as I did at that moment. I don't know how long I sat there; fifteen minutes maybe; give or take. All I know is it seemed to be quite some time. I felt sad but highly elated; both rolled into one emotion… the combination of the two, confusing – maybe – but at the same time slightly intoxicating.

I looked at my watch and realised that time was getting on and I had a long drive back down to Edinburgh ahead. Reluctantly, I stood up slowly and looked around for the last time. Even though commonsense was telling me it was now time to go, I was still loath to leave. This place held an aura that was difficult to explain. It felt safe; peaceful; heavenly even. It was as though I was standing on top of the world and I was the only one around. So it was with a feeling of sadness that I made my way back along the river bank, vowing to myself that one day – in the not too distant future – I would definitely return.

CHAPTER FIVE
THE LITTLE BOOKSHOP

Anybody who knows me well, will know of my penchant for flea-markets, car-boot sales, antique fairs and second-hand book shops. There is something obscurely interesting about sifting through someone else's unwanted possessions. You never know what bargain or little gem you may pick up! 'One man's trash can be another man's treasure' – or so the saying goes!

However, it was in the month following my trip to Dirlot and whilst taking an impulsive short-cut through the main shopping area of Edinburgh that I found my 'little gem'. Tucked away down a narrow lane, I came across the quaint little bookshop completely by chance.

The small, brass bell attached to the top of the door jingled as I opened it.

You don't see many of these, nowadays – I said to myself, quickly glancing up to the bell as I stepped inside.

The first thing I noticed was a strong aroma of fusty paper, old leather and dust. Not a particularly unpleasant smell by any means... but one that was reminiscent of most old book shops.

Sitting behind a desk just behind the door was an elderly, white-haired, bespectacled man reading a newspaper. He looked up and smiled at me.

"Hello there," he said, warmly. "Can I help you?"

I immediately smiled back. "Hi," I said. "I'm just going to have a browse. Is that okay?"

"Of course, take your time," he replied, peering at me from over his glasses. "Just ask if you need anything." He shot me another smile then went back to his newspaper.

With a quick glance around I could see it was not a particularly big shop – quite small in fact, but the number of books on display was nearly enough to fill a small library! They were everywhere! Many were lined up on shelves depicting the different genres, whilst others were stacked in small piles at various points around the shop floor. It was like an Aladdin's cave of literature… I was in my element!

The first one I picked up was a red leather-bound copy of *The Poetical Works of Sir Walter Scott* dated 1892. I presumed this to be a first edition. Illustrated and with each page edged with gold leaf – it was in excellent condition for its age. Reserving it mentally as a possible 'maybe' I placed it back on the shelf and carried on looking around.

It was the tall glass cabinet on the far wall of the shop that caught my eye. Sitting alone on the middle shelf, with a small card placed in front of it was a very old-looking, brown leather book. On closer inspection I read the description written on the card…

'French Translation of the New Testament of Jesus Christ.'

M'mm – interesting, I thought as I tried to open the cabinet door. It was locked. I looked over to the man behind the desk. He now appeared to be busy cataloguing a small pile of books into a ledger that was sitting on his desk.

"Excuse me, can I bother you for a moment?" I called, trying to sound as polite as possible.

He looked up from what he was doing. "Certainly," he said, standing up.

"This book in the cabinet – can I have a look at it, please?" I pointed to the book through the glass.

"Ah, yes – the copy of the New Testament," he stated. "Certainly you can." On saying this he opened a drawer in his desk and produced a key.

"It's all in French, you know," he informed me as he unlocked the cabinet door.

"So I see by the description on the card," I said before adding, "It looks really old."

"It is," he confirmed, handing me the antique leather bound Bible. "Published in 1699. It has the date inside."

I could see that the two very old metal clasps on the front and back cover kept the pages securely fastened together. Not wanting to damage the clasps in any way I pressed them open as gently as possible. The thin parchment paper made a slight crackling noise as I turned to the title page.

The inscription was beautifully printed in antique plate…

LE NOUVEAU TESTAMENT
DE NOSTRE SEIGNUR
JESUS CHRIST
Et publiee par l'autoite du Pape Clement V111
M.DC. XC1X.
Avec Approbation & privilige du Roy.

Mentally – and definitely slowly! – I translated it as best as I could into English and then carefully began to turn over more pages.

"It's amazing!" I remarked. I closed the book and fastened it back up in the same manner I had used to open it, before handing it back to him. "I bet it's got some history behind it. Where did you get it from?"

"An old friend of mine. His daughter brought it in yesterday with a few other old books. She said they were having a clear out. You see, I buy and sell books and I bought them as a 'job-lot'. I thought this one is a bit more special than the rest, so that is why it is in the cabinet."

I watched as he placed it back on the shelf and locked the glass door. I gave him a querying frown. "It's got to be worth quite a bit, then? I bet you it's expensive."

"Not for what you getting, it's not. It's in excellent condition for its age." He then looked straight at me and nodded his head. "If you are interested, I could do you a good deal."

"R-right," I nodded back in agreement, but sounding unsure. "I'll have to think on that one."

"Well, don't 'think' too long," he said as he walked back to his desk. "Because I believe something like this will sell pretty quickly."

Ten minutes later, I bought *The Poetical Works of Sir Walter Scott* and left.

For two days, the antique Bible was never far away from my thoughts. Where had it come from? Who had brought it to Scotland? And what year was that? These were the questions I was asking myself and once again – as in the past – I felt driven to find the answers.

The following day, I returned to the bookshop and bought it.

CHAPTER SIX
DINNER WITH A SCEPTIC

I must admit, at first, this 'new finding', did take my mind off the Knights Templar and their sacred treasure. Not gone completely, mind… just put on the back burner for a short while.

It was during a regular evening of dinner and drinks with friends in a trendy wine-bar in the dockside area of Leith, that the subject was broached again. But this time though, it brought with it animosity and scepticism. Despite having family and friends who knew and accepted my passion for the Templars and their allegiance to the bloodline of Mary Magdalene – there were also ones who didn't. Like most controversial subjects, there would always be conflicting views. You cannot expect everybody to agree with what you believe to be right or wrong. Everybody is entitled to their own opinion, so they say and – I must point out – that normally I totally agree. However, on this particular subject I found this easier said than done!

It was a warm evening, following a hot day, so after our meal we had decided to take our drinks outside to the patio area that overlooked the water. Much cooler out here, we had all agreed. We had been discussing the

Templars and their association with the Magdalene Dynasty for the past half an hour.

"Excuse me, for a moment please."

Leaning against the rail that overlooked the dock was a friend of one of the lady members of the group. She had stood up straight and looked directly at me as I passed by. I had just returned following a call of nature and was on my way back to our small group.

"It's Lou isn't it?" she asked, coolly.

I stopped and turned to smile at her. I noticed she had a glass of what looked like red wine in her hand.

"Yes that's right," I said.

"Well, Lou... would you mind very much if I ask you a question?" She smiled back at me but it was not a smile that was reflecting in her eyes.

Despite being introduced earlier in the evening, I wasn't sure of her name. I was also not sure of her abrasive attitude. I was instantly on my guard. I moved next to her and leant against the rail.

"Err... no. Go ahead." I sounded hesitant. I wasn't sure what was coming next. But first of all I needed to know her name. "I'm sorry – I didn't quite catch your name earlier on."

"It's Miriam," she replied, with an upper crust tone to her voice. "I'm a friend of Maureen. She told me she works with you and how you are in to all this Knights Templar stuff... or whatever you want to call it."

"That's right, I am," I replied, automatically glancing over to the rest of the party who were sitting at nearby tables.

Maureen immediately flashed me an eye signal as though to say... are you okay? I nodded and smiled back as if to say – 'don't worry... I'm fine' and then turned my attention back to the conversation in hand.

"I have been interested in them for a while now," I added.

"Well, what you were going on about before?" she asked, the coolness in her voice still obvious. "That stuff about Mary Magdalene and her association with these Knights? And apparently, you were also saying there is a connection here in Leith—"

"Well, there has to be," I cut in. "Have you not seen Leith's coat of arms? It's a picture of Mary... not the Virgin Mary as commonly thought... but Mary Magdalene holding a small child. Don't forget, Leith used to be the Templars' principal port in Scotland and they were her most trusted and loyal supporters. They did everything in their power to protect her name and – *especially* – the Magdalene Dynasty. So it is commonsense that she would be on the coat of arms."

Her curiosity showed in a small frown. "Magdalene Dynasty? And what is that?"

"It's the bloodline of Jesus Christ and Mary Magdalene. They had children that carried it down."

She shook her head in total disbelief. "I *don't* believe that at all!" she said, adamantly, with a short, hard laugh. "Where on earth have you got that from!?"

"Well... there are scriptures that were never allowed to be published. Missing gospels and documents that never even made it to the New Testament. Take John, for example – in one of his later works – he refers to her as Jesus' consort —"

A deep scowl etched into her brow as she cut me short. "Rubbish!" she retorted, her voice rising slightly. "I've never heard anything so daft in all my life!"

"*No*... it's *not* rubbish!" I protested. "Believe it or not... it's the truth!"

She shook her head again; her mouth in a tight line, but never said a word. I took in a long, inward breath and then looked directly at her before speaking again.

"May I ask *you* a question, now?" I said.

"Do go ahead." The response was cool, short and to the point.

"Well," I continued. "Tell me then – if you think this is rubbish, why did Jesus admit to his disciples that he loved Mary more than all others? Don't forget, it was she who he kissed on the mouth – that would only happen between man and wife. It was a different era then to what it is today. And why did she call him 'Rabbi'? In those days you *had* to be a married man to have this title. Also, why was it Mary that anointed his head and feet a week before his arrest? She would have only taken on this duty if she was his wife. And, then –

why was she given the right to attend to his body before the burial, if she was *not* his next of kin?"

She looked at me and pondered on this for a moment before giving a small, cynical smile. "Well, *first* of all – before we begin – let's get it right, shall we? Technically that is *four* questions – not one," she said, her voice and expression noticeable with thinly veiled sarcasm.

She was trying to be condescendingly superior here, but I didn't acknowledge it.

"So, I'll endeavour to answer them in turn, as best I can." She took a small sip from her glass of wine and then continued. "Right, let us go to the first question – shall we?" she said, still speaking scathingly in the third person. "You don't have to be married to be a Rabbi. Not that *I'm* aware of, anyway."

The haughty tone in her voice was beginning to get right up my nose!

"I think you'll find that in those days, you did," I cut in, quickly.

"Okay, okay," she said, waving her hand in the air, dismissively. "But because I'm not sure about that, I'll let you have that one. But loving her more than anyone else, you said...? and kissing her on the mouth...? Well... that doesn't mean she would have to have been his wife for that to have happened!"

I wasn't getting anywhere with her – I knew this, but something made me continue. "As I said before, in those days a relationship between a man and a woman was completely different to what it is now."

I could see by her expression that she still was not convinced and felt the need to explain further.

"You see," I continued, patiently. "They had customs that they stood by. If you read John's gospel you will see that she was constantly there, by his side. Some of the disciples were not happy about this; resented it even – especially Peter. He made no secret about his feelings towards her. She travelled with Jesus and was a close companion to his family. She was at the foot of the cross during his crucifixion and the first to visit his tomb afterwards. She was *also* the first to speak to him in the garden. He admitted to Peter that he loved her more than any other and called her his blessed one. She was named as being the Apostle's apostle, superior to all the other disciples' wives. She was closer to him more than anybody else. So – of *course* he loved her!"

She pulled her mouth into a tight line and shrugged her shoulders indifferently.

"Maybe so," she said. "But I still can't see that is enough proof to say they were married."

I was starting to become impatient but tried not to show it.

"*Okay…* you seem to know quite a lot about the gospels, so – if you *do* – you will know what the wifely duties were after a man and woman were married." I sounded amazingly patient, but in reality I was bordering on the point of being patronising myself.

"You will also know that to sanctify the marriage the wife had to wash the hair and feet of her future husband and anoint him with oils and then at a later date she would do the same to acknowledge the conception of a child. She would then carry the oils in a small jar hung round her neck so – if she outlived her husband – she could anoint him at the time of his burial. Which is *exactly* what Mary did."

"Yes, I *know* this," she agreed. "But it *never* mentioned that they were married."

I blew out a small sigh of exasperation. "But-you-*have*- to-read-between-the-lines, here!" I emphasised slowly. "As I said before, you *have* to take into consideration the rules of those days. *Only* – as the wife of Jesus would Mary have this right to anoint him —"

"Right – right – right!" she interjected sharply, putting one hand up as though in submission. "I *know* what you are saying, but wouldn't there be a lot more detail of this in the Bible if it was true?"

"No," I said, shaking my head. "When the New Testament was put together nearly four hundred years later many scriptures were missing and left out. It wasn't until centuries later that they began coming to light. It's in these scriptures that the truth lies."

"So what else is there about this *'truth'*?" The sarcasm was still there.

My gaze challenged hers. My reply was blunt and straight to the point.

"Mary and Jesus had three children."

She shot me daggers of disbelief. "Wha-at!" she retorted. "So what you are actually saying is – that Jesus *not* only fathered children but it was through a relationship with a prostitute… a sinner… who – if you remember – he had cast out demons!"

For fuck's sake, I thought! Just like with John the gardener, these harsh and unfair words hit home. Hard. He had defended her name and now I felt the need to do the same. 'She was *no* prostitute, reformed or otherwise,' he had said to me, angrily. I could now relate to his anger. This was such a miscarriage of justice that had tragically and ignorantly been carried down through the eons of time. I had to take in a deep and calming breath before I could trust myself to speak.

"Mary Magdalene was *no* prostitute!" I said slowly and firmly, reiterating the gardener's words. "And she certainly was *not* a sinner! She was his consort. But instead of being sainted like the Virgin Mary and the rest of the disciples, *her* good name was destroyed. Annihilated!" I marvelled at the steadiness in my voice. I might have appeared calm on the outside but I was bristling with anger underneath.

Taking another drink from her glass, she scowled at me but never spoke.

"You see," I explained carefully, believing her silence as a go-ahead for me to continue. "Jesus had to be kept pure – it went with the whole story. So as I said, when the New Testament was put together years later, many of the writings were kept out of it.

"There could be no threat to the church. No wife. No children. And therefore – no bloodline. This way they would have full control. Mary was a threat to their church and everything that it stood for. So if anything came out about a Christ Dynasty, it would turn the whole of the Catholic religion upside down. So it *had* to be suppressed… and to do this many people would be killed in the years that followed… it didn't matter how or how many… as long as the truth never came out—"

"If this is true and there *were* children," she interrupted, "I still can't see why it is not mentioned in the original scriptures. I mean, let's face it – there would have been no problem with the church then, would there?" she queried, coolly.

I was getting totally exasperated here. "But, I keep on telling you, it *was* mentioned in the original scriptures!" I argued. "As I *said* before – it was left out when the New Testament was first put together *many* years later. They – the church – wanted Jesus as a holy man with no bloodline. It was John who said in one of his later writings that Mary was pregnant with their first child when she went into exile just after the time of the crucifixion—"

"But I thought you said before that there were three children. So *if* this was her first child, how could the others have come about if he wasn't here? Did they just manifest themselves as if by magic?" Her scathing remark was difficult to ignore.

"They were born later."

Her puzzlement showed in a sideways querying frown. "But that's impossible," she said. "How?"

"He didn't die on the cross— "

The scowl on her face darkened even more. "*What*... I can't believe that! That's bloody terrible!" she intercepted angrily, before taking another drink from her glass. "Of *course* he died on the cross; that's what it's all about. He was the Son of God and he died to save us all."

I could see how upset she was becoming and I didn't want that. I had to calm the situation somehow.

"I'm *not* disputing that. I totally believe in him. And you are right. He *was* the Son of God. He was born from the line of David. *But* – He was born as a man –a *very* good man – a holy man – but still – *a man*." I told her gently, suddenly – once again – remembering more words of John the gardener from Rosslyn. "You see, unknown to the soldiers, He was still alive when they took him down from the cross. It did happen sometimes, trust me on that…"

I mused for a moment, bringing to mind the failed attempt of the crucifixion of Jacques de Molay but knew this was not the time or the place to mention this.

"And," I continued, "that is why there was no body in the tomb. Also, the scriptures say he was with them for six months after the resurrection and then left for three years before returning again. Where did he go? You have to ask yourself that!"

"There was no body because after he spoke to the disciples he ascended into heaven," came her steely explanation.

"I am sorry, but I can't agree with you on that. *If* he was on this earth as a man – wherever *or* whenever he died – whatever you chose to believe, there would have to be human remains of some sort, wouldn't there?"

She looked at me with utter disbelief. "Well… I think you are speaking a load of shite!" she exclaimed, looking and sounding indignant. "Standing there, completely disrespecting the greatest story ever told! I think it's terrible!"

I shook my head. "No, Miriam," I said quietly but firmly. "'Greatest' – yes. I can appreciate that. But not the greatest *'story'*… it was meant to be, but the powers that were then, took this and turned the 'greatest story' into the greatest lie ever told!"

That did it! I could see by her body language that she was now incensed.

"This is awful!" she scowled, shaking her head in anger. "I can't stand here listening to all this absolute drivel about him *not* dying on the cross and having a wife and children! It's just… well… it's just… heresy… sacrilege, for want of a better word!"

I was sorely tempted to point out to her –as she had to me – that this was 'technically two words' but felt that would come over as being slightly childish: petty even. So quickly dismissing the urge to one side I smiled at her sadly instead.

"You see, *I* don't class this as sacrilege or heresy," I replied. "I class it as the truth —"

"Now then you two! What's going on here?" I turned to look in the direction of the familiar voice. Maureen grinned up at me. "You are both being very unsociable. Are you having secret talks or can anybody join in?"

"No – no – it's nothing like that!" I replied with a short laugh at the same time feeling relieved of the interruption. "We were just having a bit of a debate." I glanced at Miriam and smiled but it wasn't returned. No love lost here then, I told myself!

"Well, I'm in desperate need for another drink!" Maureen continued with another wide smile. "Go on – Lou, do me a favour. Go and get me one, please." She inclined her head in the direction of the entrance to the bar. "It's bound to be packed in there and you are a lot bigger than me!"

"Seeing as you put it so nicely, how can I refuse!" I smiled, realising that I was now in desperate need of a stiff drink myself! "Does anybody else want one, by the way?"

Maureen shook her head. "No, I've already asked them…" She stopped and then glanced at Miriam, noticing her nearly empty glass. "Unless you are ready for another?" she asked her.

"No, I'm fine, thank you," her friend replied. "Anyway, I will have to go soon. I have got an early start in the morning." With this she quickly drained her glass and placed it on a nearby table.

"What are you drinking?" I asked Maureen.

"Gin and tonic, please," came the reply. "In fact," she called, as I started to walk away. "To save me going back later, can you make that a double, please!?"

"Any excuse!" I laughed, without looking back.

Maureen was right. The bar was busy. And when I returned to the table with the drinks ten minutes later, Miriam had already left.

CHAPTER SEVEN
TEA WITH A PSYCHIC

My continuing search for anything to do with the Knights Templar and the legend of the Holy Grail appeared to be never-ending. The history lesson I had given myself all those months ago, I presumed would have been over long before now. But in fact, it was just getting longer – the more I delved; the more I found! Every new path I followed would somehow always have a connection to these Knights. That is, apart from one unusual purchase that I'd had in my possession for nearly two months now. It was the small, brown leather copy of the French translation of the New Testament that I had bought on impulse from the old bookshop. Dating back to the year 1699, I could see no obvious association with this and my unfinished quest in any way whatsoever. I could only think that it must have been one of those quirky but impetuous buys that most people have from time to time. Extravagant? Probably. Especially when it seemed it would be destined to sit on a bookshelf for years to come… or so I thought…

***

"Next time you come down, bring it with you," Louise, my daughter said to me, during a telephone conversation that we were having concerning the Bible. "I'll have a look at it for you. You never know I might be able to pick something up."

At the risk of repeating myself – but in this case it could be excused as being a father's prerogative – I have to say I have two gifted children. Both in completely different ways. Paul is the artistic one. Music; the stage; photography; art and design – he has many talents. Louise's gift is foresight and mediumship. Coming from a long line of clairvoyants and with proof of going back to the soothsayer of the court of Elizabeth I, she is – according to the opinion of those who seek her services – amazing!

"When you mean 'pick something up', do you mean by holding it?" I asked her.

"Yes, that's right," her voice came down the line. "It's called psychometry. This way you can sometimes feel the vibes around an object. I might not get any, but I can try."

One week later, with the antique New Testament in tow, I made the journey down to Newcastle to visit my two children and their families.

We had just finished afternoon tea when I showed Louise the Bible. Sitting opposite me at the dining room table she clasped it between her two hands and then closed her eyes for several moments. I waited patiently, wondering what she was going to say. Would she be able to 'pick something up' as we had hoped? It would be certainly very interesting if she did!

"Wow!" she remarked with admiration on opening her eyes. "This is something else! There is so much going on here! I want you to write this down so you don't forget." She indicated her head to a notebook and pen lying in the table before looking intently at the closed book still held in her hands.

"I'm getting a lot of sadness," she continued. "A small child... a boy... about eight years old, I think. A bonny, dark-haired little thing. Hang on —" She stopped in mid-sentence, waited and then gave a small, apologetic smile. "Oh, I'm sorry," she said. "But I've just been told, he's ten... ten years old!" She paused once more and then looked at me. "A'hh!" she said with feeling. "He was *so* frightened."

"Frightened? Of what?" I queried.

She frowned and shook her head slowly. "E-rr, I'm not quite sure. A ship? A galleon of some sort," she said hesitantly.

Another short pause. Then suddenly she nodded her head as though in confirmation of something.

"Oh, yes, it's definitely a galleon," she carried on. "It's *very* rough sea. A storm of some kind. The ship is rocking and rolling everywhere! Bless him... he's all on his own!"

She went silent again – this time for a lot longer than before. I felt I shouldn't say anything; I didn't want to break her concentration.

"Yes," she said suddenly. "He's French and he's travelling on his own to Scotland. This is where his only family live, so he has to move there. His mother died along with his baby sister in childbirth. Now his father has died and he's an orphan. He had the Bible with him. I've also been shown a cross of some kind that he wore around his neck. It's different to the normal one. This has two horizontal bars on it –not the usual design." She stopped speaking again before giving me a compassionate smile.

"Ahh, poor little lad," she remarked. "He says he didn't like the boat at all! He was very sick! But… I feel as though someone *did* take him under their wing, mind. There was an older boy who looked after him."

Another silence.

Again I sat quietly, waiting for her to speak again.

"This is a family Bible," she remarked, placing the book down onto the table. "And now I have another cross here – a red cross —"

"A red cross!?" I cut in with a frown. "What sort of cross?"

"It's not really like a crucifix," she explained. "It's got more pointy bits on the ends. It's difficult to describe —"

I had to smile. "Do you mean like this?" I asked as I picked up the pen and began to draw a diagram of the Templar splayed cross.

"Yes, *that's* it!" she exclaimed, pointing to my sketch. "Well, there is a long connection with the family of this Bible and this cross. Does that make any sense?"

I raised my eyebrows in surprise. "Well, that is odd," I replied, indicating my head towards the Bible. "Because this is the cross the Templars wore on their mantles during the crusades, but that was *long* before this New Testament was ever published."

"What year was that again?"

"1699," I answered. "It tells you that inside. You see, the Order of the Knights Templar was dissolved by the king of France in 1307 – that was *years* earlier."

She picked up the book again and carefully opened the two clasps on the front. "I still feel very strongly that the family who owned this go right back to these knights, mind," she observed as she began to turn over the first few pages. "They had a history with them long before this was printed." She lifted her head to look at me. "I'm getting names here," she said quickly. "French ones, I think… Err… I think it's a Hugh?… Gerard…? a Pierre and an Andre?"

My mind kicked my senses up a gear. Whilst I couldn't place Pierre and Andre –I certainly could Gerard and Hugh – or in this case, 'Hugues'! Here were two Templar Knights. Right-hand men of Jacques De Molay

Louise's voice cut into my thoughts. "You're not writing this down!" she said, bossily pointing to the pen

I had just put down on the table. "There are so many names here; I don't want you to forget."

I quickly obliged.

"I'm telling you," she declared adamantly, watching me as I wrote the names down. "This family who had the Bible had a *really* strong connection with these names. It was a loyalty that had been handed down with each generation."

She went silent once more. I sat waiting with my pen poised ready!

"Ooh!" she began again. "I've been given the name 'Jack' here. They are saying that his enemies couldn't kill him. He wouldn't die! People are escaping. They have to get away!" She stopped and closed her eyes for a moment.

My mind had now accelerated into top gear!

'Jack…?' I thought. Surely this had to be Jacques De Molay? It had to be. This was unbelievable!

"They did kill him in the end," she carried on. "It was an awful death. There was a fire. Angry people. It's hot; it's burning!" She suddenly stopped speaking, closed the book and put it back down onto the table. She looked upset: sad even.

"This is *so* emotional," she said, pointing to her bare arms. "Look, I've got goose-bumps!"

I peered at her arms and nodded. "If it's too much you can stop, you know," I told her with a worried frown.

"No – I'm okay. I just need a breather for a minute." She went quiet yet again as though deep in thought.

"You weren't alone that day when you first went to Rosslyn Chapel," she said suddenly with a bright smile. "There was someone with you. Did you know that?"

I gave her a knowing smile. "Really?" I said, realising that she meant 'spirit' was there rather than a living person. "Funny that you should say that. Something odd *did* happen that day, actually!" I then proceeded to tell her about my strange feelings whilst in the chapel and the crypt. I didn't mention John the gardener, though. I still wasn't sure about him myself!

"Well, you definitely had company!" she assured. "You were not alone."

"Was it someone I know?" Somehow I knew it wasn't but I had to ask.

"Not a person who has passed from this life, if that is what you mean," she answered, affirming my thoughts. "I feel it is someone you have known in a previous life. I'm picking up a man – tall; quite muscular; possibly in his late thirties. Again I've got another French name for you... 'Jean'?" she said, pronouncing the name as the French version of the English 'John'. "It's all connected to the red cross. All of this might not make sense at this minute, but, don't worry it will do."

My mind, that had slowed down to a steady rate of thinking, picked up speed again.

"Jean?" I iterated. "Could that be 'John'?"

"Possibly. But I've been given the French 'Jean'!"

I blew out a long breath. This was a lot to take in. Jean or John? I wasn't sure about this. I didn't know a 'Jean', but I *had* met a very mysterious and elusive 'John', right there in the garden at Rosslyn. But surely wasn't that a bit of a long shot to assume that they were one and the same person? But then what about Pierre, André, Jack, Hugh and Gerard? Apart from Pierre and André, I could identify with them all. Just before their leader Jacques de Molay's arrest in October 1307, it was Templar Knights, Hugues de Chalons and Gerard de Villiers that organized the escape of many of the knights and their sacred relics from their Paris Temple onto sailing ships waiting to take them to the safety of distant allies. But, how on earth could Louise know all these names, my inner thoughts wanted to know? I certainly had never told her about them. And as far as I was aware this was not a subject that was generally listed in a school's history curriculum!

So there was definitely a link with the antique Bible and the Knights Templar... I knew that now. Was this why I had to go into the little bookshop right off my normal beaten path and then feel compelled to go back and buy it? Was it all part of a plan? I knew I had to investigate deeper. The man in the bookshop did say that he was a friend of the owner, so maybe he could help. I made a mental note to myself that on my return to Edinburgh – at the first available opportunity – I would go back to the shop...

In the meantime however, I would spend a pleasant evening with my son and his family. We would catch up on family news and generally put the world to rights. And then, finally – because of our mutual love of the 'beautiful game' – it would be remiss of me not to say here that there might even be a brief discussion between the two of us on the subject of football!!!

CHAPTER EIGHT
THE OLD MAN OF LEITH

Due to work commitments, it was two weeks later, on one of those dreary autumn days with grey skies filled full of fine drizzle, that I finally returned to the old bookshop.

The sound of the old-fashioned doorbell and the distinctive aroma of old leather books and dust were instantly familiar. However, the young, dark-haired man sitting behind the desk was not.

"Hi, there," he greeted with a broad grin. "Are you all right?"

I quickly returned his smile. "Yes, thanks," I replied before looking around in hope of seeing the owner somewhere. The shop was empty. "Is the older gentleman around?" I asked him.

He stood up and walked around from behind the desk. "Oh, you mean my grandfather?" he answered.

I noticed he was quite tall with an athletic build. Wearing faded jeans and a black T-shirt with 'BLACK SABBATH U.S. TOUR '78' emblazoned on the front, he looked a bit out of place in this small, antiquated bookshop. More suited to a second-hand record store or something similar, I thought!

"I'm afraid he is not in today," the young man continued.

I frowned and must have looked disappointed.

"I'm sorry about that," he said. "Can I help at all?"

"I don't think so," I replied. "You see, he sold me this book – it was a copy of the New Testament; a French translation – and I was wondering if there was any information about its history at all. It was quite a while ago when I bought it, mind."

"Ah – I remember it!" he exclaimed. "It was me who wrote the card for the bookcase."

"Oh – good!" I said, looking pleased. "Do *you* know the owner? Your grandfather said he did."

"Yes I do. He's a friend of the family. His name is Alexander Martin. It was brought in by his daughter, Margaret, I believe."

I nodded. "Yes, your grandfather told me that. You see, I think I know a *little* bit about its history but I was hoping to find out something more… maybe?"

"I'll tell you what I can do," he said walking back behind the desk. "If you can hang on for a few moments, I can ring my granddad and see if he can help you."

"Thank you. That's very good of you," I smiled.

"No problem," he said as he picked up a telephone sitting on the desk. "What's your name, by the way?"

"It's Lou," I answered. "Lou Jones."

As he made the call I began to browse along a nearby bookshelf. The name on the top of the shelf said 'Gardening and Agriculture.' Not my 'cup of tea' at all but I didn't want to appear as though I was listening into the telephone conversation!

It wasn't long before he put the phone down and called across. "Granddad says he doesn't know much about the book, but he is going to try and ring Alexander and ask him."

"Are you sure?" I frowned. "I don't want to be a bother."

He shook his head. "No, it won't be a bother. I know Alex, he is a lovely man. My grandfather said he would get back to me as soon as he had spoken to him. It might take a while, though. Can you hang on a bit longer? Maybe half an hour or so?"

I remembered passing a small café at the top of the lane. "That's fine," I said. "I'll go and have a coffee while I'm waiting." I opened the door and then turned to him. "Oh, I'm sorry," I added. "I don't know your name."

"It's Callum," he grinned.

"Well, thank you again for your help," I said smiling back. "I'll go and get that coffee then, okay? And I'll see you shortly."

Thirty minutes later, the time between entering the café and leaving it, the fine drizzle had now turned into a deluge of lashing rain! Realising that it wasn't going to pass as a shower, I had no option but to make a mad dash back to the bookshop!

"God! It's certainly coming down out there, isn't it?!" Callum commented with another of his wide grins as I entered the shop.

"You're not kidding!" I laughed, shaking and brushing myself down. "I'm absolutely soaked!"

He waited until I had composed myself and then said, "I've just this second had Alex on the phone. Granddad told him about you wanting to know more on the Bible's history and he said he would love to speak to you about it. I did say that you wouldn't be long, but he had to go. Apparently, he didn't *even* know his daughter had brought it into the shop. He seemed a bit upset about that."

Oh dear, I thought – the last thing I wanted to do was to upset anybody.

"Err'm – he doesn't want it back, does he?" I queried, tentatively.

He shook his head briefly. "No – no. I don't think so. Anyway, put it this way – if he does, he didn't say anything. All he seemed to be was really pleased in the fact that you were interested in it. He said there was too much to tell you on the phone – so maybe you would like to meet him and have a little chat. That's if it is okay with you?"

I beamed in delight. "That would be great!" I said quickly. "As long as he doesn't mind."

"He wouldn't have suggested it if he did. He said if it is convenient with you, he could meet you at his house on Sunday afternoon, about three o'clock. If it's not,

114

he'll understand. I just have to let him know, either way."

"This Sunday would be fine," I said, sounding pleased. "Where does he live, by the way?"

"Leith," came the answer. "I've got the address written down for you."

"Oh, that's handy," I remarked with a smile and then realising what I had said, I quickly rephrased my words. "Not handy that you have written the address down, but the fact that he lives in Leith! You see, I stay in a small hotel there."

"Where in Leith?" he enquired.

"Not far from the Links," I answered.

"Oh well, Alex's house is only about a couple or so miles away," Callum said as he handed me a piece of paper off the desk. "It's the address," he explained as I began to read it. "You should be able to find it, no bother."

"Thank you," I smiled. "You have been *really* helpful."

"It's been my pleasure," he grinned, affably. "Good luck, anyway. I hope you find what you are looking for!"

I thanked him once more and left the shop. The first thing I noticed was that it had stopped raining. The second – was a feeling of mild excitement at the prospect of meeting Alexander Martin and hearing what he had to say about this mysterious New Testament. Too much to tell me on the phone, he had told Callum... now that was intriguing!

***

The middle-aged lady who answered the front door to the large, Victorian terraced-house, seemed pleasant enough.

"Please come on in," she smiled after I had introduced myself. "I'm Margaret, by the way. My father is so looking forward to meeting you. Come this way, he's in the drawing-room."

The inside of the room was exactly as I had imagined it would be. Furniture and furnishings – a mish-mash of different designs from across the decades – filled every available space. Two high-backed, bottle-green leather armchairs stood each side of a tall mahogany fireplace. What I presumed to be numerous family photographs – ranging from sepia to colour; depending on the era – were placed at intervals along the mantelpiece. A real coal fire was burning in the grate. What I first noticed about the slim, distinguished, elderly gentleman, sitting in one of the armchairs, was his shock of white hair! As I followed Margaret into the room, he immediately stood up to greet me. I warmed to him instantly.

"This is Lou Jones, Dad," his daughter told him.

"Come on sit down here, lad," he said, beckoning me to the chair at the other side of the fireplace from where he had been sitting. "Come on and make yourself at home."

As I eased myself into the armchair, he looked me over quickly before sitting back down himself.

"I'm Alexander Martin, by the way," he smiled. "But call me Alex… everybody does."

I nodded in acknowledgement to him and then looked up to Margaret who was standing between us. "This is very kind of you both," I said. "I really appreciate you giving me your time."

Alex put one hand up. "Don't you worry about that," he assured me and then came straight to the point. "Well, I hear you have bought the Bible?"

I straightened up slightly. "Yes, I have. I've had it for quite some weeks now."

"We-ll," he said. "I must admit I was a bit put out when I found out it had been taken to the bookshop without my permission, mind. I didn't even know it had gone until I got the phone call." He gave Margaret an admonishing look as he spoke.

"I didn't think you were bothered about it, that's why," his daughter explained to him, coming to her own defence. "As far as I know, you've never looked at it for years. It was just lying in a cupboard gathering dust. You see," she added, turning to me, "my Dad wants to move to a smaller house – a bungalow, maybe. This place is far too big now, so we are having to down-size and get rid of a load of stuff. In cases like this you have to be a bit brutal sometimes." She then cast her eyes to her father. "Otherwise you would be hanging on to everything. I know what you are like!"

Alex gave a small shrug. "I know what you are saying is right," he agreed reluctantly, "But I would just like to have been informed that's all!"

"I *keep* on telling you that I am *really* sorry, but it's done now so there is nothing I can do about it," she said, sounding quite matter of fact.

Well, that was a bit harsh, I said to myself. I wasn't quite sure about her.

"Anyway," she added, coolly with a sniff. "I've got things to do, so I'll leave you two alone for a while. I'll bring you some tea in shortly."

As she turned to walk out of the room, Alex turned to me and pulled his mouth into an exaggerated look of feigned horror. I had to smile at him. I knew what he meant! He then waited for her to close the door behind her before he spoke again.

"Don't worry about Margaret," he said. "Her bark is worse than her bite. Anyway, in truth – she is right – I have got far too much stuff!"

"Do you live on your own?" I asked him, wondering if there was a Mrs Martin around somewhere.

"Aye – I do. My wife died two years ago and my daughter – who you have just met – and my son are married with their own homes now. It can be a wee bit lonely sometimes, but I'm lucky I suppose compared to some. They are always popping in – grandchildren included – and Margaret calls in every day to see if I am okay. You know, don't be put off by her manner because underneath all of that she has got a heart of gold really. She can be a bit daunting sometimes and definitely bossy – but she's really a big softie! It's like this carry-on with the Bible... I know she was only trying to help, but I just wish I had known, that's all." He sat quiet for a moment, looking pensively at the floor.

I gave a worried frown. I felt as though I had to say something.

"Do you want it back? I don't mind if you do," I offered politely.

He looked up and jumped straight in with his reply. "No-no-no, son! It's yours now. Margaret is right, it *was* sitting in a cupboard gathering dust. No – I would have probably given the go-ahead anyway. When I spoke to Callum and he told me how keen you were in finding out more about its history, I felt – to go to all those lengths – you must really be interested in it. And now I have met you – I like the look of you!"

He smiled at me and I quickly smiled back.

"My children aren't really bothered about keeping it," he carried on. "But with you, I can see it has gone to a good home!"

"Yes, it has!" I smiled again and then paused for a moment. Should I mention Louise and her reading, I wondered to myself? Would this be a wise thing to do? I made a split-second decision and decided to chance it.

"I think… I *might* – know a little bit about it already," I ventured carefully, watching his reaction. "You see, I don't know whether you believe in all this or not, but my daughter is psychic. She is a professional clairvoyant and medium and according to people who have seen her for readings – very good in her field, apparently!" I waited for a response.

He smiled and nodded his head up and down slowly, but said nothing.

"Anyway," I continued, noting his silence as acceptance. "When she held it, she said it had a very emotional and powerful history. She told me quite a lot about this, but I don't want to say anything yet. I want to see what you say first."

"Fair enough," he said. "Well, firstly I have to say I don't disbelieve in what your daughter does. I'm open-minded about it. Margaret's the one who loves anything like that, though. She is always getting tarot readings. She swears by them! Me? – I'm open to debate!"

He then paused, narrowed his eyes slightly and looked at me with a curious smile. "So you want to know whether our two stories tally up, do you?"

"Er-r, no – not really… well… yes, I suppose I do in a way," came my conflicting response. "I just know I felt a strong need to buy it and now I have I would love to know more about the history."

"Well," he said, leaning back in his chair. "It's certainly got lots of that! And your daughter is right…

it's both powerful *and* emotional!" He took in a deep breath and then blew it back out very slowly.

I waited in anticipation. Something told me this was going to be good!

"Right," he said. "Firstly, let's go to the Bible coming here to Scotland. It was brought over from Rouen, in northern France, by my great-great-great-great grandfather, Jean-Pierre Martin. He was just a wee boy at the time. His father had not long died and his mother had also died in childbirth along with his sister, five years prior to that. Tragic really! The only family he had left was an aunt and uncle who lived here in Leith, so his guardians in France had to organize for them to take care of him – not an easy task getting messages back and forwards in those days, I can tell you! It all had to done by ship and then by post-boys or stagecoach. This could take months. Finally, after making sure there would be someone at this end to meet him, they put him on a merchant ship that was leaving Rouen for Scotland. It makes you wonder what he must have been thinking. It must have been awful for him! Poor, wee man!"

His face clouded over and his voice faltered a little. I watched as he leant over to the fireplace and picked up a poker from the hearth and began prodding the fire with it.

Jean… Pierre…? My mind pounced on these two words immediately. M'mm, I thought, interesting!? Louise had mentioned the two names separately but I had presumed them to be different people. So, maybe this was not the case. However, she had also mentioned the small, orphaned boy and the sailing ship! This was definitely a good start!

"When was this?" I questioned, once Alex had settled back into his chair.

"February, 1741," came his reply. "Apparently, according to family history that's been handed down, it was terrible weather. There was a violent storm…"

Storm!? I quickly brought Louise to mind again and mentally ticked a box.

"…he was in a dreadful state. Terrible seasickness! He was very frightened!"

I gave him a short, knowing smile. "I can completely associate with that!" I said, strongly, swiftly recalling a horrendous ferry journey I had experienced when stationed at RAF Saxa Vord.

"Oh, dear!" He gave a sympathetic look. "Are you not a good sailor, then?"

"Definitely not!" I went on to tell him about my RAF posting to the Shetland Islands in the early 1960s and an unforgettable sea-ferry journey onboard the *St. Clair*. "There was one time," I recalled. "We were on our way to RAF Buchan near Aberdeen to play football, when we hit the tail end of a hurricane – Hurricane Flora it was called. It was a nightmare – what with that and the fact that we'd had quite a few drinks in Lerwick before we set sail, I thought I was going to die! I've hated sea travel ever since!"

122

He gave a small chuckle. "Well, you and Jean-Pierre had something in common, then! According to our family history, this particular sea voyage put him off for life too! He never put a foot on board a ship again! Luckily though, there was a young man on board that looked after him."

'Someone taking him under his wing,'… Louise had said.

Check! Another tick!

"It was a young laddie from here in Leith," Alex pressed on. "John Hastie was his name. He was eight years older than Jean-Pierre and had been sent to Paris two years earlier to take an apprenticeship in stone-masonry. He had just completed his course and as chance would have it he was now on his way home. It was John that handed Jean-Pierre over to his aunt and uncle who were waiting here at Leith when the ship docked."

"Was Jean-Pierre the owner of the Bible, then?"

"Originally, no. It belonged to his grandfather," he replied. "Along with a Cross of Lorraine that had belonged to his father, these were his most treasured possessions. I still have the cross and I am *definitely* hanging on to it!" He then added with a determined grin, "Margaret can say she's 'downsizing' as much as she wants! She's not getting her hands on that!"

"A Cross of Lorraine?" I queried. I'd heard of it but I wasn't quite sure what it looked like.

"Aye, it is variation of the traditional Christian cross," he said. "I'll try and explain it you about it as best I can!"

I sat forward slightly in my chair. This guy can really tell a story, I said to myself!

"Originally it was called the Patriarchal Cross and was supposed to originate in Eastern Europe in the ninth century," he narrated. "It was also the arms of the Patriarch of Jerusalem who granted its use to a religious order of knights during the first crusade. It was a leader of this crusade – a Godfrey of Bouillon, Duke of Lorraine – that used it as his standard when he took part in the capture of Jerusalem. The cross was then passed down to his successors and so became the Cross of Lorraine. It was the symbol of the French Resistance during World War Two and is still used in different coat of arms all over the world to this day. It has two horizontal bars going across instead of the standard one bar. This represents the emblems of spirit and earth together by combining the square earth cross and the cross of Jesus Christ —"

'Two horizontal bars going across?' My thought cut in quickly, the penny suddenly dropping – Louise had said this when describing the cross belonging to Jean-Pierre.

Another tick, I thought! I was feeling quite pleased with myself here!

I then said out loud, "I think I know a bit about this cross. Is there not a connection with it and Mary Queen of Scots? Is this the same one?"

He nodded and smiled. "Yes, you are right – it is. This was through her mother, Marie de Guise, who we know as Mary of Lorraine. It was on her coat of arms." He paused for a few seconds and then continued with his story. "Now then," he said. "Where was I? A'ah, yes – I remember; Jean-Pierre meeting with John Hastie."

"This is the young mason?"

"Aye, that's right," he said. "According to my father, my great-great-great-great grandfather, Jeanne-Pierre and John remained friends all their lives." He paused and contemplated for a moment and then gave a little smile. "I think I've got the number of 'greats' right there," he said, drolly. "It's very important you know!"

"I'm sure it is!" I agreed with a smile. I then asked him the same question I had asked Louise. "The French 'Jean' is the same as the English 'John', isn't it?"

Alex nodded again. "That's right," he said. "In this case, it's a Martin tradition going right back to the fourteenth century that every first-born son to be called – Jean. Well, Jean-Pierre actually. Obviously – now, because we are in Scotland, it has been changed to John – John Peter."

"Who started this tradition?" I enquired.

He leaned back in his chair and peered at me through half-closed eyes for a moment. "Okay, laddie," he said, looking serious. "I'm going to tell you a story..."

I sat silent: totally engrossed.

"The tradition started right back in the year 1308 when a wee, baby boy was born in Paris. He was named after two very brave knights – his father and uncle: Pierre and Jean. They served alongside a greatly respected man of that time called Jacques De Molay..."

I sat upright in my chair. I couldn't believe this! I was on fire! Once again, Louise had been spot on. She had now ticked all the boxes, as they say! Her clientele were right – biased or not – I have to agree with them... she is amazing!

"I know all about him!" I declared brightly. "I've been interested in him and the Knights Templar for ages now!"

Alex looked pleased. "Well, if that's the case," he said. "You'll know that he was the last Grand Master of the Order and that he died at the stake in Paris in March, 1314 – nearly seven years after his arrest."

I gave a brief nod of the head. "Yes, I do. I have been living this for three years now." I paused for a brief moment before speaking again. "You know before when you mentioned the knights who carried the Cross of Lorraine during the crusades?"

"Aye."

"These were the Templars, weren't they?"

"They were," he affirmed with a nod. "As you will probably know, they've had a lot of bad press over the years but this was originally fabricated by their enemies – King Philippe IV of France being the main culprit. It was he who poisoned the Pope's mind against them with his lies. You will more than likely know as I do, that they were courageous and honourable knights, who fought for integrity and truth and more importantly believed in the Dynasty and bloodline of Jesus Christ. Many were persecuted and perished because of this faith…"

Don't get me started on that one, I said to myself…

"And," he carried on, an unbridled passion obvious in his voice, "although they were more often associated with their own cross pattée or the rosy cross… the one that they wore on their tabards and shields… many of the Templars that had been arrested and captured the same time as Jacques, etched the sign of the Cross of Lorraine on their cell walls while awaiting their death." He frowned and shook his head, slowly as he continued. "These were totally unlawful and 'fitted-up' charges against good, brave Christian men and resulted in – what some historians refer to – as 'one of the worst crimes in medieval history'!"

I nodded my head in total agreement. "I know," I said, sadly.

"Well, our family – the Martins – can be traced back to these times," he continued, with a trace of pride in his voice. "I know it's been mainly verbally from generation to generation, but sometimes that is the best way." He paused for a moment as though regaining his train of thought and then continued. "So, let's go back to little Jean-Pierre who came here in 1741. It was his twelve generations past grandfather, Pierre – if you know what I mean? – who, along with his brother Jean, served Jacques de Molay. When Jacques was arrested, Pierre stayed in Paris to support his leader whilst Jean – the younger by a year – was given orders to help sail their fleet away from France and to safety. Jean was on one of the sailing ships that came here to Leith. He finally settled in the village of Temple and became very close to the Sinclairs of Rosslyn who – you will probably know – owned the castle and then later – the chapel."

"Yes, I know this," I confirmed, nodding my head. "I have been there a couple of times. It's a lovely place!"

"It is indeed!" he agreed, wholeheartedly and then continued. "Well, according to family history, Jean aided Henry Sinclair and Robert the Bruce at Bannockburn. Henry, by the way, was the Sinclair who was the signer of the truce to achieve peace between Scotland and King Edward II of England. After the battle, Jean went on to marry and raise a family. Pierre – however, was not so lucky. Following his arrest, he and many other knights were tortured and then executed. However, his wife was pregnant at the time of his death and a son was born six months later. So, in memory of his late father and his uncle, he was named Jean-Pierre Martin and then the name has been carried down to each first born son – generation to generation.

Luckily, there has always been a boy in each one; so the tradition has never ended."

I was totally immersed in the whole story.

"What happened to Jean?" I wanted to know. "Did he have any children?"

"Yes, he had two girls later in life, but he never lost touch with his French family he left behind. Especially his brother's and his namesake – the first Jean-Pierre. Because he had two girls, the Martin name stopped here in Scotland – that is, until 1741 when wee Jean-Pierre with the Bible came here."

He glanced across to me. I was trying to take everything in as best as I could, but he could see I was struggling to keep up.

"Complicated, isn't it?" he smiled.

"Just a bit, but I think I'm getting there!" I nodded. "So this little boy – your great-great-great-great grandfather," I then said slowly, mentally making sure I got the number of 'greats' right as I spoke. As Alex had pointed out before – it was very important that you did! "He must have had a son to carry this family name down..." It was really stating the obvious but I had to make sure.

"Aye, that's right."

"And then his son had a son to get to your grandfather." Another mental count... I think I've got that right, I said to myself!

"Aye," Alex confirmed. "As I said, generation to generation. But in 1825, when my great-grandfather was born, they decided to change it to the English – John Peter—"

"But your name is Alexander, isn't it?" I said quickly, wondering that if this was the case he must have an older brother.

"I am the younger of two sons," he replied, confirming my thoughts. "My brother was called John."

"Was?"

"Aye," he replied, solemnly. "He passed away last year. He was born six years before me in 1914. I've got an old photo here of him."

As he stood up to reach a framed photograph of the mantelpiece I eyed him curiously and did another quick mental count. 1914… six years younger… 1920 then…? That must make him about eighty-three, I mused. Because of his build, agility and sharpness of the mind – he certainly didn't look his age!

"Here," he said, handing me the photograph. "This is the two of us together in 1945 – just after the war." He waited until I looked at it. "See," he remarked, "We've got our demob suits on! I'll tell you what; it was nice to get back into civvies again!"

I glanced up to him. "You were in the armed forces, then?" It was a statement rather than a question.

"Aye, we were both in the navy. John was in the 'Royal' and me the 'Merchant'."

"You must both have been good sailors, then!" I remarked, drily. "Unlike little Jeanne-Pierre!"

"True!" he laughed. "Mind you, we went through some pretty rough seas, but you didn't have time to think about it. Keeping Hitler and the 'Jerries' away was enough to distract you from anything!"

"I bet it did!" I remarked with a grin and then cast my eyes back down to the black and white photograph. Two young men – one fairer and shorter than the other – were standing side by side. The taller one of the two's hand was on the other's shoulder. Both hairstyles were slicked back with a side parting: very much in fashion for the day.

Alex leant over and pointed to the taller man. "That's John," he said.

I looked more closely. The dark-haired man reminded me of someone. The strong jaw line; the long nose; the wide mouth... they all looked strangely familiar.

"I seem to recognize your brother from somewhere!" I remarked with a questioning frown.

"Oh, most people say that about him," he said, as he sat back down in his chair. "He was always out and about; he loved walking – he did it for years. He was a well-known figure around here."

Still staring at the uncanny image, I shook my head. "I *don't* think so," I frowned in puzzlement. "You see, I haven't lived here for that long. I'm not from around here."

He gave a small, bemused smile. "I sort of guessed that!" he said. "Now, let me see... you sound like a Geordie, right!"

I nodded and grinned again. "Aye... and a true one at that! Born on the banks of the Tyne!"

I turned my attention back to the photograph. Recognition suddenly dawned! Maybe it was just a fanciful thought but the face that was staring up to me reminded me so much of John the gardener!

"How old are you here?" I asked, stretching over to Alex to hand the photograph back.

"M'mm, let me see," he answered staring at the picture. "John would be about thirty and I was twenty-five."

"You were quite fair when you were young – compared to your brother, that is."

He grinned and pointed to his mass of white hair. "I had blond, curly hair then and loads of it too! Definitely not fashionable in those days, so I used to flatten it down with Brylcreem! Do you remember that? You being a 'Brylcreem boy' and all that?!"

I had to laugh. "That was a just a bit before my time, like! But yes, I can remember it!"

"Oh, I'm sorry," he said, with an amused look of surprise. "It's okay; I *can* see you are a wee bit young for those days. I was only joking! No offence taken, I hope?"

"Definitely not!" I said with a smile.

He stood up again and placed the photograph back onto the mantelpiece and then sat back down. "No, John was the dark-haired one," he continued. "He was much taller than me as well… a true 'Martin', in fact. Me… I take after my mother's side. She was a 'Hastie'… Ann Hastie."

"Wasn't 'Hastie' the name of the young mason on the ship?" I quizzed.

"Aye, that's right. John Hastie. As I said, our families have been friends ever since then – one way or another. My father, John and my mother were childhood sweethearts. They married in 1914 just before the outbreak of World War I. Just like his father and grandfather before him, he served in the Royal Scots. A sort of family tradition, you might say! He was sent to fight in northern France just after John was born. My son, however was like you… he joined the RAF in the '60s and then his son did the same twenty years later…"

All military men here, I thought. But then taking into consideration the family history and pedigree, it goes without saying that I wasn't surprised!

The sound of a clatter of crockery came from a distant room through the house and broke into our conversation.

Alex cocked his head in the direction of the door. "Oh, dear," he joked. "It sounds like Margaret is smashing up the happy home! She's obviously making some tea. You will stay and have some, won't you?"

I glanced at my watch to check the time. "Yes, that would be nice, thank you. But then I'll have to get back," I said, not wanting to outstay my welcome.

"Do you have far to go?"

"No – just two or three miles away," I replied.

"Oh," he said sounding a little surprised. "So you stay in Leith, do you? And here's me thinking it's Edinburgh."

"No – Leith," I confirmed. "I have a room in a small hotel near the Links. The head office of the company of where I work is in Edinburgh."

He nodded in acceptance and peered at me, a twinkle in his eye. "And you're a Geordie!" he concluded with a smile.

"Yes, I'm a Geordie!" I said, smiling back.

***

Later, as I drove through the dark streets of Leith on my way back to the hotel, my mind was racing; pounding questions at me – one after the other. Alex had been amazing. This remarkable old man had told me more than I could have ever imagined about the Bible and its history. Everything he had said I could associate with – one way or another – and all Louise's findings had been recognized and confirmed. So, all in all it had been a very educational and enlightening afternoon.

But… there was something that still puzzled me or to be more precise, I should say 'somebody'. It was somebody who had puzzled me from the day that we met. It was John – the gardener from Rosslyn Chapel. Who the hell was he? Why could he not be accounted for? He had told me that he had a long connection with the Sinclairs – but for how long? He said his family had come to Scotland in the early fourteenth century. Was this the year 1307? But did they? Maybe… it was *not* a family that had come here but one lone person. And not as a voluntary immigrant, as he had led me to believe, but as escapee fleeing from his enemies. He had told me that he knew everything there was to know about the Knights Templar. Was this just plain arrogance on his part or was it firsthand experience? He had appeared from nowhere and then disappeared without a trace. I knew I hadn't imagined him – he was not a figment of my imagination.

And, I was so certain I knew his face. Had he recognized me in the same way I had recognized him? He was so sure about the spelling of my name. He didn't have to ask – he knew he was correct. And talking about names; what about his? He said he was called John – but now I knew 'John' was the English translation of 'Jean'. So, 'John' or 'Jean'… it didn't really matter. What did matter, was where he had come from. Past or present; he must belong somewhere. The staff at Rosslyn had never heard of him. Well, maybe he had never been there? Not in this lifetime anyway.

And what about the old black and white photograph of John, Alex's brother? It had bore such a strong resemblance to him. So in this case, would it be slightly insane to believe that John the gardener and Jean Martin, the fugitive knight who – with many other Templars – had fled his native country in order to protect their fabulous treasure from their enemies, not to be one of the same!? What other reason could explain his earthly – or should I say unearthly presence?! And is this why I felt so sure *I* had met him before? Not present day but in a past, different life, maybe? I had heard of re-incarnation – obviously, but until now the 'doubting Thomas' in me had always been sceptical about it. Now, I was beginning to accept that maybe there was something in this after all. Maybe previous life experiences can exist, I told myself. Because let's face it, recent events had surely given me strong evidence of proof that they do!

I was now convinced that this was why I had felt compelled to buy the copy of the French New Testament and then seek out its history. The outcome of my meeting with Alex, the old man of Leith had – once more – brought my persistent quest back to the Knights Templar. Ever since my first visit to Rosslyn, I had experienced this unaccountable pull towards these valiant knights. Why? And, why did I feel the need to protect their name and everything they believed in from sceptics and discreditors?

There must be a purpose here, I mused as I drove the car down the avenue next to the links. A reason behind all of this. But, I still wasn't sure what or why.

Yes, everything was falling into place, but there was still something missing; the journey was not quite over. The final curtain could not ring down...

...not yet anyway.

CHAPTER NINE
SECRET SYMBOLS AND DEGREES

As I travelled the length and breadth of Scotland with my work, the legend that is the Knights Templar and the Holy Grail continued to follow me around. My camera was always close at hand; my eyes never stopped looking – churches and chapels with Masonic crosses and signs; ancient castles and buildings with emblems, inscriptions and artefacts, were all there in abundance.

Many sceptics would have you believe that their presence in Scotland has been romantically over-played, but on this comment I would have to disagree. There is too much evidence of this out there for their presence to ever be denied. These honourable Knights bore the Templar legacy with pride and despite the decimation of their order in 1307, they were determined to keep this legacy alive right through the centuries up to the Masonic orders of modern day. The proof is out there for even the most hardened of cynics to see.

Once more – to quote 'John the Gardener' – you just have to know what you are looking for!

In the meantime, I absorbed every piece of information I could find. And just as John told me in the gardens at Rosslyn – and hopefully without the risk of appearing arrogant – I can honestly say that there wasn't much I didn't now know about these knights. I learnt about their history, beliefs, habits and lifestyle. But more so, I became fascinated in their use of a secret and ancient geometry around which they planned their maps, architecture and directions. The Knights Templar were believed to be the inspiration of a host of these Masonic symbols and degrees and none so much as their revered 'number three'.

Still used by masons of modern day, this degree of the sacred geometry – the highest level being that of 'thirty-three' – was applied extensively to the levels of freemasonry, architecture, layout of buildings and last – but certainly not least – in the longitude and latitude of their esoteric planning of maps and charts. Used in securing positions for their bases, prefectures and headquarters throughout the world, three degrees – either singular or in multiple terms – crops up far too many times to be that of a coincidence.

However, little did I know that at this period in time, this magic little number would play a major key role in finding the answer that I had been searching for so long now. The final piece of the jigsaw – so to speak.

And so, as the months and seasons rolled by, the reasons and wherefores of this unexplained and intense interest that I had now adopted about the Knights Templar and their sacred treasure continued to elude me. Surely there wasn't much more information to be found; because I was now like a walking encyclopaedia of Templar activity!?

So why could I not let it go?

The only answer I could give myself was that I was looking for a closure of some sort… but closure of what? This was what I couldn't quite work out.

So my search carried on regardless. Relentless and untiring. I just knew that this was unfinished business and I wasn't giving up.

CHAPTER TEN
CROSS OF LORRAINE

It was in late March of 2007 and the offer of a new position of a concession manager in an upmarket department store in the heart of Scotland's capital city, was too good an opportunity to turn down. However, this would mean that instead of driving around the highlands and lowlands, I would be now spending most of my time in Edinburgh. Not an unpleasant prospect at all – I told myself! After years on the road and living out of a suitcase it would be nice to sit back and slow down just a bit and take life at a much more steady pace! Maybe it was this pending finality of my travelling that explained the sudden and impromptu need to pay a much overdue visit to a certain place one more time.

***

Tucked away in an isolated area of the northernmost county of Caithness, with its funny little 'castle-that-was' and the darkly named waters of 'Devil's Pool', stood the curious graveyard that housed the stone statue of the mysterious Lady of Dirlot. Having made several insurance calls to this remote county over the past months, it was a place that – despite a 'half-forgotten about' promise to myself that one day I would – I never did return. On these previous visits I would always find an excuse... 'not enough time'... or... 'maybe next time'. Regrettably, now – in hindsight – I should have ignored these lame excuses. I was well aware of that now. So therefore, I knew that if any insurance claims were made from this northern part of Scotland before leaving my current job, in order to fulfil that promise, I would have to make time!

***

As luck would have it, two weeks before leaving for my new post, I was given a list of three insurance claims for Caithness – all of them around the town of Thurso.

It would be a two day visit; the plan being that the first day would be taken up with the claims and then spend the night in a hotel. The following morning, after a quick look around Thurso town and its little curio shops, I would then – hopefully – have enough time for a quick visit to Dirlot!

It was mid-morning on the second day when I made my way down Thurso High Street. With all the calls completed, I now had a few hours to spare before driving back to Edinburgh.

Despite the spring sunshine, there was a definite chill in the air and as I had finished earlier than expected I felt a cup of coffee would be a good idea before the long journey south. The small tearoom on the other side of the street looked ideal.

As I walked across something caught my eye. Directly in front of me, fastened to a tall, metal pole, was – what I presumed to be – a coat of arms. Enclosed in an oval seal, with a silver and black background, was the noted picture of the en-haloed Saint Peter with the keys to heaven in his right hand. Nothing unusual about that – you might say – apart from the fact that in his left hand where he would normally carry a staff, he held the Cross of Lorraine.

Strange? – I thought, as I looked up at the coat of arms. I wonder why that's there?

This was something I had never seen before and I stood for a few moments trying to work out the significance.

"Excuse me, it's Lou isn't it?" A vaguely familiar voice cut into my puzzled thoughts.

I turned swiftly round to face the smiling face of Elizabeth, the wife of Charles Stuart from Loch Calder.

"Hello, there!" I said, returning her smile with a large one of my own and sounding pleasantly surprised at the same time. "It's lovely to see you again!"

"Same here," she said. "It's been quite a while, hasn't it?"

"Aye, it has. It must be getting on for four years, surely?"

She nodded. "Yes, it must be. Time flies, doesn't it?"

"Definitely!" I agreed with another smile.

"I thought it was you crossing the street," she said. "I had just dropped the newsletter of at the office when I saw you and I had to come over and say hello."

"I'm glad you did," I told her. "I was about to go and have a cup of coffee when I noticed this." I pointed up to the picture of Saint Peter before turning to look at her. "I'm a bit puzzled here. Maybe you can tell me why he is carrying the Cross of Lorraine instead of a staff?"

She gave a short laugh. "You are not the first person to ask that," she answered. "I can only tell you what I know, mind." She paused and then continued, indicating her head in the direction of the small café. "Listen, did you just say you were going for a coffee? Because I quite fancy one myself. If it's okay maybe I could join you?"

"Of course it is. It would be a pleasure!"

Ten minutes later we were sitting with our coffees next to the window of the tearoom. It was traditional in a quaint sort of way. Small vases containing an assortment of silk flowers were placed in the middle of a half a dozen or more pine tables covered with red gingham cloths. Around the room, historical pictures of Thurso and the surrounding areas adorned the walls. It was typical of a market town café.

After taking a drink from a white china coffee mug, Elizabeth placed it back onto the table and leant forward slightly.

"Well," she asked with a smile. "You want to know about the coat of arms, do you?"

I nodded, picking up my mug at the same time. "Yes please. It has got me a little bit baffled." I paused in order to take a drink of the coffee before continuing. "Do you not think it is strange that Peter is carrying the Cross of Lorraine in his left hand? Is there a reason behind this?"

"I'm not sure what you mean by 'a reason'," she remarked with a puzzled frown.

"Okay," I replied. "Why is he holding the Cross of Lorraine? Is there a connection with that and Thurso?"

"W-well, I don't believe it is actually meant to be portrayed as the Cross of Lorraine. It's not registered as that, anyway." She sounded unsure. "You see, in this case it symbolises the two-barred cross or – to give it its proper title – the Patriarchal Cross. The reason Saint Peter holds it in his left hand opposed to the pastoral staff is because he is classed as the Father of the Christian church – or in this case – The Patriarch. It was during the first crusade when one of the leaders, Godfrey of Bouillon, the Duke of Lorraine commandeered the cross when he was made ruler of Jerusalem. This was a title he didn't want but the cross was a different story. He adopted this as his own. Hence – the name the Cross of Lorraine—"

Aha! I knew this story! "But didn't the Knights Templar use it first?" I interjected.

She nodded her head and smiled. "A'hh," she said with a touch of intrigue in her voice. "You know about the Templars, do you?"

"Just a wee bit!" I said with a grin, pretending to play it down.

"Well, yes, you are right. They did use it. It was granted to them for their use by the Patriarch Of Jerusalem. They carried it to the first crusade."

I quickly brought to mind how Alex Martin had told me about this.

"Yes, I know," I said to her. "I knew it was used in the crusades. This is why I know it better as the 'Cross of Lorraine'."

"The Patriarchal Cross was actually first used in Eastern Europe in the tenth century and still is, even to this day. The top bar represents the crucifixion and the lower one – the resurrection. It's because of this that Catholic churches world-wide use it as a symbol for their faith."

I took another slow drink of coffee and absorbed what she was saying.

"Oh – I see," I said, thoughtfully as I placed the mug back down on the table. "Well, which cross is the one on the coat of arms here meant to be – the Patriarchal or the Cross of Lorraine?"

"I'm sure it is the 'Patriarchal'," she replied. "According to the local historians, anyway. But – there are connections both ways. The actual design goes back to the seventeenth century to when Thurso was appointed a free burgh of barony by a charter signed by King Charles the *First* of *England.*" She then picked up her coffee mug again and took another drink.

I followed suit, immediately noticing how she had put a slightly derogatory emphasis on the words 'first' and 'England'.

Is this for my benefit, I thought? Or is it just for the English in general? I wasn't sure on that one! With a married name of 'Stuart' and a maiden one of 'Sinclair' and born and bred here in Caithness, wasn't there just a trace of the old 'Jacobite Rebellion' floating about here!? With my mouth hidden behind the coffee-mug, I had to press my lips together in order not to show a smile.

"It happened when he came to Scotland for his coronation in 1663," she continued. "Don't forget that he was a Protestant but his paternal grandmother, Mary Queen of Scots was a staunch Catholic. She also had strong links with Lorraine from her mother, Mary of Guise or – as some history books refer to – Mary of Lorraine. Also, because my family – the St. Clairs or 'Sinclairs' – as we call ourselves nowadays – owned extensive land in Caithness at the time, they would more than likely have had some say in the design. There is proof of this with the silver and black background. This alludes to their engrailed coat of arms."

"Yes, that's right!" I said, suddenly realising I had missed the significance of this detail. At the time I had been too intrigued with the cross to notice. "So, if that is the case, there is a possibility that this cross could represent the Cross of Lorraine and not the Patriarchal Cross as registered?" I queried, my train of thought being that of Sinclair's connection with the Templars and then these knights' connection with this cross. It seemed logic somehow.

"She gave me a guarded smile. We don't know for certain, do we?" she said, cautiously. "But I can see where you are coming from."

There was a short pause. "Were those leaflets I gave you of any interest, by the way?" she then asked brightly, completely changing the subject and her tone of voice.

"Yes, they were. Thank you." I quickly went on to tell her about my trip to Dirlot with the Devil's Pool and the arrow-shaped graveyard with its mysterious stone statue. I was going to tell her of my plan to go there after leaving the café, but there was something else I had to mention first. It was something that had been puzzling me ever since my first visit.

"I couldn't help thinking that this was a rather unusual place to build a castle," I remarked. "It's strange, isn't it?"

"What do you mean – 'strange'?" The wariness was back in her voice.

"Well, there is nothing there for miles around, is there? It's in the middle of nowhere. So why on earth would anybody want to build a castle there?"

I noticed her eyes glazed over guardedly as though she was weighing me up. It was as though she wasn't sure of my motive for asking this question. She paused for a moment before she spoke again.

"It was built by the head of a very famous Scottish family in the early fourteenth century," she said. "His name was Reginald de Cheyne. He was a great chieftain and – at the time – held a lot of sway here in Caithness. Actually, it was not a castle as such, even though it is called that. It was originally built as a keep. Soldiers were billeted there. A bit like a garrison, really."

"But why?"

Picking up her coffee, she looked at me over the mug. Raising her eyebrows, she gave me an ironic smile.

"And why not?" came the dry response.

There was more to this than she was letting on here. I felt as though she skirting around everything I was asking her... and I wanted to know why.

"It's just seems a bit odd to build a castle – in such a far-flung place like this – just to keep soldiers in. I mean, what were they doing there? What was their purpose?"

"Reginald de Cheyne didn't own the castle for very long," she said, seemingly still ignoring my pertinent questions. "When he died it was taken over firstly by the 'Gunns' – another powerful clan of the time. Allegedly James Gunn was a Templar himself and a friend of one of my ancestors –William Sinclair. It was the 'Gunns' who added on the cemetery at a later date as a burial ground for the family."

"Yes," I said. "It's an unusual shape, isn't it?"

"That's right, it is," she agreed. "It's a five-sided figure – like a pentagon. This is a shape used a lot by Masonic builders. It's like the tombs in the cemetery. Apart from the family ones, you might be interested to know there are unnamed ones there too. These are etched with the Masonic markings of the skull and crossbones."

"Ah, yes," I said, quickly jumping in. "I saw those. I thought they were bones of some sort, but I couldn't quite make them out for definite as they were so old. So they *are* the skull and crossbones, eh? This is associated with pirates as well, isn't it?"

"Yes, piracy is our modern day idea of the symbol. But let's not forget it is also used in military units, colleges, organizations right across the globe and – of course – as a warning for toxic substances. But originally it had a sacred meaning. It symbolised the place of the crucifixion and immortality of Jesus Christ. For this reason, many Knights Templar used this on their tombstones and I think you will find this is what has happened at Dirlot."

"Right," I said, now realising that there was definitely a Templar influence here. "It will be interesting to look at them again." I pondered on this for a moment and then continued with my original line of questioning.

"Getting back to the castle," I said with a slightly, insistent tone in my voice. "I *still* for the life of me can't understand why they had a castle there in the first place. Howay man, it wouldn't be used for defence, would it?! I mean, what was there to defend!?"

"What was there to defend?" She threw the question straight back to me.

This was the second time she had done this. Was she playing for time?

I carried on, regardless, "Aye," I persisted. "Why build it in such a remote spot?"

"In those days the clans were always doing battle with each other," she remarked. "Especially the 'Gunns', the 'Sutherlands' and the 'Keiths'. So they always had to be ready for an attack. The keep had a very open aspect in the way of seeing their enemies approaching."

"M'mm," I thought, not at all convinced. She was evading my questions and I wondered why. I wanted to ask her this but out of respect I refrained from doing so. Instead I said out loud.

"I'm thinking about going back to Dirlot today, before I leave for Edinburgh. And I want to take some photographs while I'm there. This might be my last chance for a while as I am changing jobs soon."

"R-right – but there isn't much to see, is there?" She sounded puzzled.

"You're right, there isn't, but photography is a bit of a hobby of mine plus the fact I found it a really fascinating place. It had a weird feeling about it… sort of spiritual in a kind of way. I had a very similar experience a while ago when I went to Rosslyn Chapel. That place is truly amazing!"

"I've heard people talk about this," she nodded, knowingly. "And I totally agree. But you have to remember I'm a 'Sinclair', so you will probably understand when I say that I am a bit biased here! I just love the old place!" She gave me a bright smile before adding, "But, tell me, what happened to you?"

I proceeded to tell her about the strange events that I had experienced during my first time at Rosslyn. I told her about the strange feelings whilst in the chapel and then in the crypt and – after what had started out to be a curious visit to an interesting and historic place – how it had now changed the pathway of my life.

And the meeting with 'John the Gardener'? No – I didn't mention that. I kept that to myself!

CHAPTER ELEVEN
MYSTERY OF DIRLOT

The seasons might have changed but the place certainly hadn't. Apart from the lack of leaves on the trees, Dirlot was exactly how I remembered it. As I walked by the edge of 'Devil's Pool', I had to look down. Notoriously dark and dangerous, its waters seemed much calmer than last time. Hypnotic even. So much that it held my attention for a few moments.

I wonder what treasures you hold, I mused to myself? What so-called 'monsters' are down there that guard it so fiercely?

I gave a small chuckle at my mental ramblings and made my way up the grassy mound in the direction of the stone-walled cemetery.

The old metal gate gave its familiar rusty creak as I opened it and stepped inside. The four unnamed graves that stood in each corner were where my immediate interest lay. There was something I needed to see again. I needed to look at the Masonic markings etched into the headstones. Smooth and eroded with age, on my first visit, the inscriptions had been barely legible. But, because I now knew what I was looking for it was so much easier to make out the roughly engraved symbol of the skull and crossbones. My mind immediately flashed back to the earlier conversation with Elizabeth Stuart in the café. She had said there was a possibility of Templars being buried here and now with the evidence right in front of me, she obviously – without a shadow of a doubt – knew what she was talking about!

I couldn't have left the graveyard without checking out the kneeling, stone statue of what I now affectionately call, the Lady of Dirlot. Still covered in lichen-moss and grime from centuries of exposure to a brutal and unforgiving climate, I hadn't realised on my first visit how neglected and in desperate need of restoration she really was. But, still she watched over the wall; hundreds of years down the line – purportedly guarding the treasure of the inky black waters below. As I photographed her from all angles, I knew that there was something about this ancient statue that fascinated me. Who had carved her from stone? What mason or masons were responsible? And… for what reason and when?

These were the questions that were still running around my head as I left the old cemetery and made my way up to the rocky mound that used to house the small castle. From here the panoramic view of the countryside made me realize that Elizabeth was right yet again. Well, in one respect, anyway. For defence reasons alone, it certainly would have had the advantage of having an open aspect on all sides. But – as I quickly reminded myself– apart from that and as far as I was concerned, that was all it had!

I was still quite disconcerted about this as I walked away from the rocky tor and headed towards the large flat stone where I had previously taken a rest before the long journey south. Yet again – call it an 'age thing' or whatever – all this tramping about and climbing up and down was certainly wearing me out! So now, for the same reason as last time I was glad to take a breather and sit down once more on my makeshift seat! I began to look around, at the same time taking in the familiar ethereal atmosphere. If you could bottle this air up here, I thought; you would be set to make a fortune!

The pale March sunlight shone through the bare branches of the trees and I had to squint slightly from its glare in order to see. The absence from the foliage gave the area a much wider feel to it and unlike on my first visit, the graveyard was no longer hidden from view.

What I noticed first was the statue, appearing high above the wall, her head looking over her shoulder. It was then cold realization took me by completely by surprise. I realized she wasn't – as previously presumed – watching over the fabled sunken treasure of the Devil's Pool. Her gaze was directed to me or – should I say – to where I was sitting.

With its colour not native to the area and long embedded into the grassy verge, was the large, flat, strangely-shaped stone…

My mind went into overdrive and I took in a sharp intake of breath. And then, just like in the chapel and crypt at Rosslyn –whatever happened to me there, was happening now – here at Dirlot. Once again, I instinctively knew I wasn't alone. A 'green-fingered' friend, possibly? Who knows. But whoever it was... the presence was undeniably there. Hauntingly, distant maybe – but definitely – there.

A wave of what seemed like a host of emotions all rolled into one swept over me. I felt weird and spaced out; honoured yet humble; completely out of my depth but totally unafraid.

I must have sat there for what seemed hours but in fact it was only minutes; my whole being now totally engulfed by the emphasis of it all. And then, as quickly as they came, the feelings and the presence suddenly faded and disappeared leaving behind an eerily stillness of awe. For the first time in seven years I now felt at peace.

Whatever the purpose or reason had been or whatever or *whoever* had brought me here to this place, I now knew it was to be no more. The magnetic pull I had felt towards searching out the truth about the legends of the Knights Templar and their beliefs was now over.

All I had to do now was to go back and try and make sense of it all!

CHAPTER TWELVE
JOURNEY'S END

If one is led to believe as I do myself, that the Holy Grail and the mysterious, sacred relics do exist and were brought to Scotland via the Knights Templar, is it not plausible to also believe that, because of the unjust disbandment of their Order and their impending arrests which resulted in many of these knights to urgently set sail from Northern France in 1307, they would not have had enough time to plan and secure a suitable hiding place for their precious cargo?

Their immediate and foremost concern would be to transport the sacred relics away from France and its greedy and unscrupulous king as swiftly as possible. The rest would have to be arranged at a later date once they had safely arrived and settled in Scotland. Here – with support from the St. Clairs – their tried and trusted allies – they would be able to bide their time in securing this place. It would have to be remote and covert; safe enough to keep their treasure protected from their enemies and marauders. They would have been well aware that finding this place would take precision and secrecy on the highest level, as in their care was something that far outweighed any monetary wealth.

They knew that its safe keeping was paramount beyond compare.

Therefore, taking everything into consideration and then acknowledging the Templars' love of the ancient cartography based on the Masonic measurement of three degrees, is this not what they would have used in the search for the site for the final resting-place of the biggest prize of all? Based on this theory and possibly risking derision from many sceptics – both academics and non-academics – after much painstaking deliberation, I believe that this is how they comprised their map…

…Firstly, using a chart of the British Isles, we begin in Somerset, England and in the small town of Glastonbury. Early accounts of the Christian conversion in the British Isles claim that it was Joseph of Arimathea who travelled here not long after the crucifixion. Joseph is described in the gospels as a rich and respected counsellor and an older uncle and disciple of Jesus Christ. However, modern-day findings suggest that at this time in biblical history, his name was more than likely titularly incorrect. Joseph – or Yosef, meaning 'to add' – of Arimathea was the Davidic Hebrew title given to the eldest son next to the heir, whatever their personal name. This title would therefore have been bestowed on James, the elder of Jesus' three younger brothers. Because of 'Joseph' and his involvement in the spreading of Christianity throughout the lands in the alleged thirty years that followed the time of the crucifixion, surely his age must have been that of a young man and not one of advancing years as we have been led to believe? This certainly makes sense!

Presuming now that Joseph/James are one and the same person, it is not surprising that it was he who arranged with Pontius Pilate to take possession of Jesus' body in order to take it to the family tomb and prepare it for burial. Now being the eldest son, this procedure would be accepted as normal practice. Lore also relates that it was James – who we must now, for the record's sake, refer to as 'Joseph' – who had in his possession the Holy Chalice that Jesus used to serve the wine at the Last Supper and which later captured and stored his blood at the time of his crucifixion.

Legend now supplies us with the rest of the story. It is widely chronicled that Joseph accompanied Philip, Lazarus, Mary Magdalene and several other apostles on a preaching mission to establish Christianity throughout Europe. On landing in southern France, Lazarus and Mary, stayed in Marseilles, whilst he and the others travelled north.

It is said that Joseph achieved his great wealth through the metal trade and because of this had probably visited the South West of England in search of tin and other metals on several occasions. In its day, Cornwall and Somerset were well-known throughout the Roman Empire for their vast source of tin and high quality lead. Because of his knowledge of these parts, it would have been only natural that he was chosen to lead the missionaries to bring Christianity to the most far-flung corner of the Roman Empire – the island of Great Britain.

Intertwining myths with historical facts, it is reported that Joseph first travelled around the coast of northern Cornwall heading for his old mining haunts, but his boat ran ashore at Glastonbury Marshes and he and his followers climbed a hill to survey the land. The name of the hill was the now famous, Glastonbury Tor.

Folklore would also have us believe that it was at the foot of this hill where he buried the sacred cup which had captured the blood of Jesus Christ. Weary from his toil, Joseph, then thrust his staff into the ground and the following morning a strange thorn-bush pertaining to the flora of foreign climes had suddenly appeared! Shortly after this, a spring – appropriately named the Chalice Well – flowed water out of the ground and according to this legend gave those who drank from it – eternal life.

The most enduring of all of the legends regarding Joseph of Arimathea, is that it was on his instruction, a small church was built here at Glastonbury. Made of wattle and daub it is traditionally known as the first Christian church in the world to be built above the ground. Used as a Celtic Monastery for many years, it wasn't until the early seventh century that the Saxons – now converted Christians – founded the now world-famous, Glastonbury Abbey and it was their King, Ine of Wessex that lay the first stones. It now stands in ruins. The Lady Chapel of the abbey however, marks the location of the original wood and wattle church and for this reason gaining the site the rightful title of 'the holiest earth in all of England'.

Today, with its famous ruins and well-documented history – be it lore or fact –Glastonbury is now a main haven for pilgrim seekers from all over the globe. Magical and uniquely spiritual, unequalled to any other place in England, it is a place of a mystical force of ley lines and unexplained energies. It is the place where Christianity in Britain began...

Now, returning to the map of the British Isles, it is my poor man's assumption that the Knights Templar applied the aforementioned form of map-building in the search for a secure hiding-place for their treasure.

And so, in hope of emulating this method correctly, I drew a vertical line starting at the sacred site of Glastonbury up to the Midlothian village of Rosslyn. Let's not forget that it was here on their arrival to Scotland, the Templars were reported to have left their secret relics in the safe hands of the St. Clairs – their longstanding and trusted allies.

Continuing with this line, I proceeded up to the town of Thurso on the northern coast of Caithness before re-tracking a few miles back down from the finish of the line. It was here I added a horizontal bar across the vertical one before travelling further south until reaching the site of Rosslyn. Again, I added another horizontal bar. Now I had the shape of the two-barred cross or more commonly known as the Patriarchal Cross. However, in this case given the history behind the keepers of this 'treasure' and the object of their mission, I would like to, from now on – in respect of their name and beliefs – refer to this cross as the Cross of Lorraine!

Now they have to search for a safe and hidden place. A place well off the beaten track; tucked away in the middle of nowhere; a place far away from their enemies and would-be treasure-seekers. Here, on the northernmost horizontal bar of the geometric line – with great trepidation, I have to ask myself – was this place found?

Secluded at a bend on the River Thurso and where the cliff reaches forty feet up from the river bed, is the site of Dirlot Castle. Now ruined to the extent of just a few remnants of the traditional Caithness stone, surely this must be the most mystifying and baffling castle in Scotland for size and defence purposes? However – even more mystifying is the unusual shaped cemetery situated near to the castle's ruins. Built in limestone, this ancient, walled burial ground is in the shape of a pentagon or – as defined in local literature and heritage sites – the shape of an arrowhead! It was this burial ground that was the main reason that drew me to the Dirlot in the first place.

Instinctively, I had felt there was a connection here; something much more significant than just a curious style of design. Was this to replicate the same design as the most important castle belonging to the Cathars of Languedoc – the ill-fated Chateau de Montségur? Let's not forget, it was here – with these devout and humble people, who preferred to pray outside in the fields without all the indoor ornate trappings of the church – that the Templars had entrusted their sacred relics for so long.

That was, however, until the atrocities of March 1244. The year when the whole of Christendom took in a breath of horror and shook their heads in disbelief.

Egged on by King Philippe II of France, Pope Innocent III instructed his army to destroy these defenceless people. Bar a few lucky escapees, the whole of this peace-loving nation was wiped out because of their non-conformist beliefs and principles.

So, it is here in this area of Southern France, standing on a high, precipitous, limestone tor, that we have the famous Castle of Montségur. Hewn out of the same stone as the rocky height and surrounded by remote, rolling countryside and marshland – it cannot be overlooked that the layout of the castle is this unusual design of an arrowhead.

Then, on the other hand, we have the site at Dirlot. With its remote, bog-filled countryside; the sheer, rocky peak and the limestone, arrow-shaped burial ground – albeit, all on a miniscule scale in comparison to the mighty fortress – is it not strikingly obvious that all the similarities are there? Are they much too relevant to disregard? *And* – if they are not, were the castle and the cemetery at Dirlot really built to emulate the Cathars' stronghold? If they were, is there a significant reason for this? Or, as so many times before, was this just another coincidence?

It was at this stage in my quest for the truth regarding the Templars' involvement with the safe-keeping of the sacred relics, that I had to recall my trips to this remote site, tucked away in the desolate part of the county of Caithness. Drawn to it by a chain of events and some unexplained force, it was here I had to pause for a moment and wonder...

Outside of the cemetery, embedded into the side of the grassy slope that looks down to the Devil's Pool – with its colour and texture not local to the area – is the large, flat stone. It was on here that I found a much welcome resting-place during my previous visit. It was also here that I had felt a sudden surge of realization. Whatever I had set out to accomplish all those many months ago; whatever this 'mission' had been about, I now knew it was nearly over – and all because of a change in the seasons...

...On that early spring morning, whilst sitting on the stone and observing the view, I had looked through the bare branches of the trees. This time, unlike my first visit in the full-bloom of summer, it was now possible to see the walled cemetery with the mysterious statue of the lady clothed in ancient robes kneeling high on the inside of the wall. Unkempt and anonymous for so many years, I had felt the need to give her an adopted name.

The 'Lady of Dirlot' she became –and in my mind she always will be. But who really is she? What is the importance about her anonymity? Nobody seems to be able to answer these questions.

Unlike most graveyard statues that stand in guard over tombs, she is looking out over the cemetery wall, seemingly watching over the ground below. Isn't there something baffling about this position? I believe there has to be.

Putting aside the theory of protecting the treasure from the bottom of the Devil's Pool, I now had to think again. It was the lack of foliage on the trees that had suddenly given me room for thought. Was there anything else there for her to watch over? In my humble opinion only – yet again, I believe there was…

…With her hands crossed lovingly over her chest as though at peace, she is looking over her right shoulder; her eyes directed to the large, flat stone…

CHAPTER THIRTEEN
CONCLUDING THE QUEST

At this point in my story, I would like ask the reader that if they have any doubts on the existence of the Templars' 'sacred treasure' and – even more so – that its presence and other holy relics are here in Great Britain, then to suspend this disbelief for a just few moments and consider the facts.

Firstly, why did the Knights Templar come to Scotland in the first place? Their presence has been proven in many parts of Britain but none so much as that of Rosslyn Chapel.

Founded in 1446 by the St. Clair family – as they were then known – it was reportedly built on the site of a much earlier church. The St. Clairs or – to give them their modern day title – 'Sinclair', were undisputedly supporters of the Templars and reputed trustees of holy relics, so it makes complete sense that the present day chapel is full of evidence predating to their activity. The multiple engravings, inscriptions and symbols engraved into its walls all reveal and confirm their descent from these knights. So, now aware of this obvious Masonic influence here, is it not surprising that the ground plan of the chapel bears a striking resemblance to the ground plan of the Temple of Solomon in Jerusalem...?

...During the first crusade, it was here that the Templars held the trusted position of keeper of the keys and also whilst excavating beneath the foundation discovered a 'big secret'. It would be this 'secret' that would clear the name of the most wronged and misjudged woman in Christian history and then – rightfully – shatter the foundation of Catholic church and turn everything it believed in, on its head. Men would be mystified and thwarted about its whereabouts for aeons to come. But – on the darker side – as the centuries moved on, this sacred treasure would also become the object of greed and fanciful promises of power to those who own it; instigating heinous crimes to be committed in order to gain its possession.

So, with the Knights Templar and their association with the holy relics and the old Jerusalem Temple, we also have the Sinclairs and their staunch loyalty to these knights and their cause. Therefore, weighing up this close link between the two, is it not plausible to wonder if the similarities of the lay-out of both Temple and chapel are not by accident but from design?

Just another coincidence you might say.

But, if that is so, why is there so much evidence in the chapel of symbols and engravings relevant to the Templar legend?

Why do burial stones carry their name?

Why at the junction of the Sinclair's own engrailed cross etched in the vaults of each bay of the main chapel and arching across the vault of the crypt below, is the subtle presence of the distinctive splayed cross of the Knights Templar?

Does this not indicate that the Templars and the possibility of their 'secret treasure' came to Rosslyn at some point? And – even if it isn't there now – surely this chapel plays a major role in the longstanding quest for the Holy Grail and other sacred relics? Even to the major sceptics – here is a place so steeped in Templar history and lore that this cannot be denied!

Secondly, what was it that led the knights to Caithness – the most remote and desolate county on Scotland's mainland? And, why does the town of Thurso show Saint Peter holding the two-barred cross instead of the pastoral staff in his left hand on its coat of arms? Local history of the area is vague about the origin of the significance and depict this as being the Patriarchal Cross. However, considering the Templars' obvious presence in the cemetery at Dirlot and with William St. Clair, founder of Rosslyn Chapel being granted the first Earldom of Caithness in 1455, maybe this is not a true description. Identical to the Patriarchal cross and held in great esteem and revered by each and every Knights Templar, could this cross in question – I ask you – not be the Cross of Lorraine?

Then we have the small, lone castle at Dirlot. Nowhere else in Scotland is there another built in such a similar location! So, with the risk of continually repeating myself – really – what *was* its purpose?

My argument for debate is from the defence point of view. There was, and still is, nothing around for miles! No nearby town or village to watch over; no coast to defend from invaders from foreign lands. Nothing. Just bleak, uninhabited, bog-filled moor land. It was brought to my knowledge that maybe its purpose was to defend the castle and surrounding countryside from invading clans. At the time, I couldn't argue with this explanation due to respect for the narrator of the story. Now, with this person no longer present, maybe I can elucidate on my simple theory? If there had been no castle there in the first place, would there still have been a reason to invade!?

Acknowledging this theory as being perfectly logical, I now had to stop and take stock of the evidence before coming up with a conclusion.

If there was no obvious purpose for the presence of this small castle, could there be a more obscure reason for it being there? Because what else could there be to defend or watch over? With the surrounding bog marshes and craggy mounds and the limestone burial ground uncannily resembling the pentagonal geometry of the Cathars' mighty castle was there not another connection here? Albeit, size-wise on a much smaller dimension than the site at Montségur, was Dirlot not the ideal area for the Templars to house their secret treasure?

Accepting this speculation as being both plausible and logical, I then had to ask myself – how did they do it?

Using their esoteric charts, did they align the longitude and latitude of Dirlot to the sacred grid system? On this instance, based on religious sites and cryptic geometry, did they apply this method of map-planning by using the Masonic level of three degrees? Commonly used world-wide by masons – past and present – many of their orders, sites, headquarters and buildings are based, built or located around this magic number – sometimes duplicated or even triplicated.

Therefore, whilst accepting that there was strong evidence of Templar presence at Dirlot and still using this Masonic geometry, it cannot be ignored at where it stands on the meridian grid system. Is it of no surprise that measurement of the 'Longitude West' at the site of Dirlot stands at the infinite number of 3.333333...°!?

So many questions; all waiting for answers. Then there are the coincidences; too many to mention here.

However, on this subject I have been informed and led to believe by an experienced, psychic acquaintance that there is no such thing as a coincidence. And I quote...

'What appears to us as a chance happening is not necessarily so. Synchronicities do not happen by chance... Somebody – either physical or spiritual has made them happen. They are meant for a reason.'

Wise words? I believe so. But, yet again, this is only my amateur and modest opinion. So, as with all the other unanswered questions, I will leave them up to you.

Maybe you can decide.

EPILOGUE

Some years ago, in the year 2000, – being a relative stranger to Scotland – I began my quest into the history behind the Knights Templar and the mysteries that surround them. I studied their allegiance to the Bloodline of Jesus Christ; their passionate belief in the preserving of the good name of Mary Magdalene and – subsequently – their legendary, sacred treasure.

My journey, which started off as a mild and curious interest soon developed into a relentless and insatiable need to find the truth. I began to read many books on the subject; scour reams of relevant literature; visit places with a Templar connection and take an abundance of photographs!

These days, I spend most of my time in Edinburgh and as I look down out of the window of my room situated on the top floor of a small hotel, I can see where the river meets the sea. The Firth of Forth. The same river that saw the Knights Templars' fleet laden with their treasured cargo, sail up her waters over seven hundred years ago. In the fading evening light, when the city lights are dancing on the dark water and if – using your mind's eye – you look really hard, you can just about visualise their ghostly presence! A peaceful and thought-inspiring vision.

As the third millennium progressed it has been from this room with a view that I have slowly tried to piece together this enthralling, two-thousand-year-old enigma.

During this time, I gleaned and absorbed as much knowledge on the subject as I could lay my hands on; no page was left unturned. I became a 'mine of information' – which I must admit, came as a bit of a surprise as this is not like the 'real me' in any way at all. This was something definitely not inherent with my character! But it was like a drug: addictive and mind-consuming. I had to read everything to know everything. Somehow I had to try and make some sense of it all, no matter how long this would take.

Now my journey is nearly over and I can sit back and contemplate on all my findings.

Over recent years there has been much speculation about the final resting-place of the Holy Grail and other Holy relics. Maybe there are many. There are certainly numerous detailed theories to verify this. Some maybe plausible and some maybe, not.

However, it is at the site of Dirlot on the River Thurso in Caithness that my quest comes to a close.

If – and I must put an emphasis on the word 'if' here – my layman's geometrics are correct and this is a sacred spot, then one must agree that 'whatever' – or dare I say – 'whoever' is buried beneath, it has been a long, difficult and covert journey to get there.

Until all this happened: this experience; enlightenment; journey – it doesn't matter how it is described but, in this case I believe the word 'journey ' to be appropriate – I was never a religious person. As previously stated – an agnostic or a modern day 'Thomas' definitely, but never one that took the Bible seriously. But now I can honestly say I have never felt so close to God as I did on the days of my visits there.

Remote and ethereally tranquil, it is truly a spiritual place.

A place that invokes all kinds of unexpected emotions.

It is a place filled with awe and respect... and in my humble and sincere honest opinion – perhaps –fit for the bloodline of a King.

After Thought

As I stand by the Stone at Dirlot
I see your statue standing tall.
Your hand across your heart,
You look at me over your right shoulder.
I whisper to myself,
It's all right, I know your story,
The legend of the pool
About the gold and treasure
Keep people away from his grave.
His cathedral is beneath the stars.
The Cathars would approve.

LOUIS LLEWELLYN JONES

Printed in Great Britain
by Amazon